*A Word Fitly Spoken*

This is number _____ of a limited edition of 300.

*Kenneth Mills, August 28, 1980.*

*Cedar Haven.*

# A Word Fitly Spoken

## Kenneth G. Mills

Sun-Scape Publications, Toronto

Other books by Kenneth G. Mills:

*Given to Praise! (An array of provocative metaphysical-philosophical utterances)*

*The New Land! (Conscious Experience beyond horizons)*

© Copyright 1980, Kenneth G. Mills. All rights reserved, especially the right of reproduction in whole or in part in any form without written permission, except in the case of brief quotations utilized in critical articles and reviews. Published by Sun-Scape Publications, Box 793, Station "F", Toronto, Ontario M4Y 2N7, Canada.

ISBN 0-919842-05-4

Printed in Canada by The Naka Press

# Contents

|   | Acknowledgments | 8 |
|---|---|---|
|   | Editor's Preface | 9 |
| 1 | A Word Fitly Spoken | 14 |
| 2 | Thoughts and the Divine | 24 |
| 3 | The One Activity | 30 |
| 4 | Be Still . . . | 40 |
| 5 | Moment of Consciousness | 44 |
| 6 | Identity and Individuality | 56 |
| 7 | Riding the Beam | 70 |
| 8 | Only One Consciousness | 78 |
| 9 | The Quest of Questioning | 82 |
| 10 | Franciscan Interlude | 96 |
| 11 | The Picture Presentation | 112 |
| 12 | Moving Furniture Around | 120 |
| 13 | "My Blasted Intellect!" | 132 |
| 14 | Equality | 154 |
| 15 | How Do You Do? | 158 |
| 16 | "I Have Overcome the World" | 170 |
| 17 | A Moment's Celebration as Easter | 182 |
| 18 | Foundation of Vision | 194 |
| 19 | The Electrical Force Field | 202 |

# *Acknowledgments*

      I wish to acknowledge the people who assisted in bringing *A Word Fitly Spoken* to the public. A word certainly seems *simply* spoken in light of all the work required to record it! These people are: Jaan Koel, who assembled and edited the manuscript, and who oversaw and contributed to all stages of production and design; Jocelyn Van Huyse, who assisted in editing and production; Susan Alberghini, who proofread the page proofs; Beverley Tudhope and Ian Tudhope, who contributed to the book's design and production and who assembled the final artwork; Ian Jaffray, who assisted in the final assembly and executed the cover design; Lloyd Harrison Jr., who printed the book; David Nash, who helped to organize and oversee production; Teresa Stevens, Linda Roedl, Mary-Gretchen Limper, and Eleanor Mills Nickerson, who typed numerous drafts of the manuscript; Pier Paolo Alberghini, Ian Tudhope, and Jaan Koel, who provided the photographs.

# Editor's Preface

Everything in the universe is singing. It is an endless, all-encompassing song, from atom to star. The essence is music, the essence is vibration, and the whole symphony of creation follows the Hand of a Master Conductor moment to moment. The Score is hidden to us. It is a mystery. Yet, from time to time we are granted a glimpse into the Unknown. This occurs when we contact a man who strives to unite his faculties with the Infinite and emerges as its instrument. The greatest music of all occurs when such a man attunes himself to the grandeur of the Divine and then gives it expression. He is an instrument plucked by Spirit, and his audience is the whole of humanity.

*A Word Fitly Spoken* contains a collection of nineteen talks by Canadian philosopher and poet Kenneth G. Mills. He has dedicated his life to illustrating how Consciousness as it IS, pure and unadulterated, is the single, most fundamental Principle of existence. The discipline that has made Kenneth Mills the sensitive instrument that he is came through his own inner searching (which included Christian Science) and his extensive music studies. He worked diligently for twenty-three years to become a concert pianist, and succeeded. He played his last concert in 1962. Shortly thereafter, a profound revelation led him to engage a higher form of Music, that of the Spoken Word. He has often told his students how well his search for the Divine was complemented by the tremendous mental dexterity garnered from his music discipline. The two eventually combined in such a way that he has since been able to still the personal, thinking phase of consciousness to the extent of allowing the Universal Music of Truth to flow forth freely in language.

The public phase of Mr. Mills's work and Teachings began in 1968, and the lectures that constitute *A Word Fitly Spoken* are only a few from a library of over fifteen thousand recorded hours of speaking. They have been chosen and assembled in such a way as to present an enlightening, comprehensive survey of the author's work since it began over twelve years ago. They range from the early years up to the present, and provide examples of both private and group meetings.

The word *Unfoldment* has a very special meaning in Mr. Mills's life. It is the word chosen to describe his Teachings. The word also describes well his life in general. His lectures or talks are called *Unfoldments,* an apt title because that is simply what happens. He never knows beforehand what he is going to say, yet his speaking always seems characterized by the planning of a well-designed musical composition. Alongside his profound metaphysical eloquence, Mr. Mills has developed a tremendous sensitivity to the conscious attitudes and states of the people to whom he speaks. He allows his *revelationary* words to flow almost of themselves according to the nature of this perception. Since these various conscious states occur in everyone at different times and in different ways, his Unfoldments are universally attractive and meaningful. When he speaks, it is evident that a greater force than mind as we ordinarily experience it to be is at the helm, guiding the course of his words. Consequently, everyone present receives something of inspirational value that relates directly to his level of awareness and capacity to understand. The pinnacle of the author's spontaneous giving of praise looms high in his poetry. In fact, many Unfoldments have come forth entirely in verse, as much as three hours at a time!

      Kenneth Mills attunes himself to the *event* of communion and communication, to the inner needs of his hearers, and not merely to the intellectual assimilation and synthetic restatement of any particular dogma, philosophy, or religion. It is evident in his Teachings, however, that many recognized religions, philosophies, and their related practices, both past and present, from Christianity to Buddhism to Judaism to Platonism, are established for the Truth they represent and provide. Albeit too that Mr. Mills does not hesitate to point out what he sees as possible areas of ensnarement amid any of these formalized systems. Hence, regardless of his intellectual or religious background, every hearer who is open-minded and sincere about his own spiritual potentiality may receive an inspiring introduction into a new perspective of life and consciousness—the initial, indispensable harbinger of *Unfoldment.*

      An invaluable gift is offered to every receptive hearer. That gift is the awakening of reverence for the Divine, which in my estimation constitutes the very seed of the new, spiritual body of consciousness that is waiting to birth. With an ever-deepening feeling of awe and wonder for the Spiritual, for the present Principle of God, the inspiration offered in the Unfoldments or any authentic expression of Reality is magnified and provides the aspirant with the necessary lift of mind and heart to elevate his awareness to a greater recognition of What IS. The deep feeling of reverence becomes the shield and buckler to any and all life situations. In times of sadness or in times of joy, it is the ever-constant pulse within that reminds us of Life's essence, eternality, and indestructibility.

*Unfoldment* embraces a variety of human interests. These interests have become very expansive and have culminated in a program of worship, enquiry, and artistic endeavor that all of its students find exciting and deeply rewarding. The activities include: instruction (formal weekly Unfoldments; numerous weekly and week-end workshops throughout the year; the annual seven-week Summer Festival of Light, Peace, and Sound held at Sparrow Lake, Ontario); music (the philosopher-poet is also a composer and conductor who leads the exciting musical activities of The Star-Scape Singers, a professional vocal complex of students who sing and record his spontaneous poetry in dynamic, modernistic arrangements); the arts and performing arts (he has participated in, assisted, or sponsored various student projects, including weaving, dance, and theatre); architecture (Mr. Mills has originated and shared many innovative building and renovation designs); business (his students operate several small businesses, all of which were originally encouraged by him). In working with his students, the author has not only displayed a remarkable ability for drawing forth their latent talents, but has actually provided them with abundant facilities, funds, and inspiration with which to realize them.

Despite the wide range of involvement that arises around the Unfoldment and how absorbingly enjoyable it is to those who participate in it, the fundamental Premise or Principle on which this unique way of life is predicated is never forgotten in the minds of its students. The Premise is encapsulated in two seed statements. One is by Mr. Mills and the other one is from the Bible: "Consciousness is fundamental and what you are conscious of constitutes your experience," and "I and my Father are one" (John 10:30), on which Mr. Mills continually elaborates: "... *now* and *not shall be* one!"

Simply stated, the practice that inheres in this work involves watching one's thoughts, words, and actions to ensure that they conform to the Ideal. The Ideal is to let life be lived on the foundation of Principle. The triads of *thinking, being, and doing* and *thought, word, and deed* are seen as the means of both exploring and expressing the above Premise-Principle. It is expected that a river, when traced in the opposite direction of its flow, will eventually express the mystery of its origin to the dedicated explorer.

The realized Man of Light, the Man of Understanding, whose Identity may manifest in the role of Teacher or Guide, is both river and Source simultaneously. Having found the Source for which others search (who on the most part do so unconsciously), he offers his thoughts, words, and deeds as the ever-refreshing waters of Wisdom. By following his stream, the student is inspired to follow his own and trace it back to its Primal Origin in Consciousness.

Everyone is searching for that Spring, for that Consciousness, for that ultimate fulfillment in Source unification. Those who are searching for it consciously are the known disciples of the Light. The rest search, but do not know that they search. They are searching unaware. The single hint that tells them there is something yet to be found is a deep feeling of unrest or dissatisfaction. The searcher's only hope at this point is that of contacting a Teacher who is himself awake, and who can awaken him to the mechanics of his hitherto unconscious yearning and its attendant suffering. When a man is thus awakened, he has been given one of the greatest of gifts.

Many aspirants find that as they begin moving with a greater sense of purpose, they begin to present challenges to other people. Yet, whatever the reasons for contention, the understanding that *everyone* is ultimately on the same search for happiness and peace, whether he knows it or not, brings solace, strength, and compassion to the heart of the aspirant. When this becomes widely understood and accepted, even those who would criticize may undergo an unmasking and period of revelation, which if deep enough, can cause them to join the very ranks of those who are *conscious* in their pilgrimage to Self-realization. This pilgrimage begins with self-awareness and the systematic application of sound philosophical and religious practices.

The Teachings of Kenneth G. Mills provide such an opportunity, and his new book bountifully illustrates this. *A Word Fitly Spoken* provides invaluable instruction in the basics of developing a practical, metaphysical view of the universe. This book, as the title suggests, is an event of profound metaphysical eloquence. This eloquence is both prose and poetry, which combine to offer a verbal music that is attuned to the Universal Symphony of Being. It is performing at this very moment—how will *you* respond to His Baton?

Jaan Koel
December, 1979

## A Word Fitly Spoken

*Remember,
you must come to a point
in your experience
when you can be
whatever anyone wants you to be
while you remain centred
in what you really are.*

# 1    A Word Fitly Spoken

June 13, 1968, Toronto, Ontario

It is interesting to see how your various questions arise, because as you ponder their arisal you may arrive at a level of comprehension where you can discern the level of consciousness that you are on. The waking consciousness is such a superficial one and that's why you are not happy with it.

> Dennis M.: I'm not sure sometimes if I really know myself as well as I sometimes think I know myself.

A very important question. Perhaps a more important way of getting at this is by asking not so much "Who am I?" but "What am I?" What are you doing right now?

> Dennis: Thinking.

Right. Thinking is usually considered an attribute of Mind, and Mind is a word for God. Thinking is the most tangible evidence of God to the seeker of Truth. It is the only experience that is entirely non-matter. People say it is localized in the brain, but the brain is merely a receiving station for thinking, so to speak. Thinking has never been found in the brain. When you stop and think, you realize that the brain itself is a thought!

> Dennis: I've sometimes thought and even felt that I am really not confined to this body.

No, and if you are not confined to this body, then you are not confined to the time sequence in which this body seems to move. What is body?

> Dennis: Matter.

It seems to be, but actually if the body is to have an identity at all, you must be conscious of it, and what you are conscious of constitutes your experience. You see, consciousness is fundamental, and if consciousness is fundamental, you know that it is only in consciousness that you can experience body. You, I, or anyone does not really experience a physical or material *body* as such. We are actually, in fact, only aware of the *idea* body. The notion that the body is material is itself an idea. The body is a manifestation of a series of ideas, a conscious experience, and people mistake it and believe it to be material.

With the realization that the body is really a series of ideas (that is, a conscious experience) comes also the awareness that these ideas, which constitute the experience of body, are contained in Mind. Mind always evidences itself as consciousness. That's why we say that consciousness is fundamental, because as long as you are conscious, you will always be embodied. You will always have that body that is necessary for you at the time you seem to need it. It will be one that fulfills its function wherever you seem to be.

An idea, you see, arises in essence from its Source in Consciousness, and that Source is unutterable and unnameable. And people usually get fooled when they think they are talking about things or ideas, because they invariably project whatever it is that they are talking or thinking about into an objective sense or framework, which they believe is outside themselves, but which in reality all arises within themselves, that is to say, from within consciousness.

> Dennis: Descartes said, "I think, therefore I am." But can you say that thinking is really the proof of existence?

It is only the proof of existence on the level of observation that says you exist on that level. It is not completely accurate. It's an educational statement. The whole point here is an awareness of metaphysics whereby you may raise the thought to such a point that you free the thinker from the belief that he is a thinker thinking thoughts, which frees his intellectual equipment from taking over and sending forth a verdict that is untrue about the status of the real Man.

You see, through our educational system we are taught erroneously about most things. Things themselves, for instance, are fine and dandy, but the burden comes from how you think about them and what your concept is about them. It's the same with the body, and it is the same with that which says, "I think, therefore I am." When you are able to declare "I am," it is rather wonderful, because this is an indication that "Where I AM, there may ye be also." You see, without the affirmation of the I AM, there is no correct identification for that which thinks it arises.

    I know that you are starting on an adventure that is extremely exciting. What is taking place is a reordering and a readjustment of your entire set of values, which has been inculcated into you for so long. And you see, the healing or the correct adjustment of any situation doesn't come about through analysis primarily, because analysis never heals. The healing takes place in the recognition that there is nothing to be healed. To confront error is to give it all the support it needs to continue its supposititious existence. It confronts everyone in some form or another and will try to get to you in whatever way it can. For instance, if you see a friend or a neighbour or someone you don't know very well who says, "I don't feel very well," you say, "Too bad." You are not affected. But if your mother and your father start complaining, you say, "Hmm, how can I help you?" You start recognizing it. First you thought it was someone else's experience, and before you know what's happened, it becomes yours. It tries to become yours because it says, "If I can make this bright fellow think that I am real, I'll have a place in his world." But little does this satanic influence realize that this confrontation has already been met and dealt with as far as you are concerned, because the promise still stands: In the I of God stands Man.

    You must realize what is really taking place on the deeper levels of consciousness in what appears as our little talk. You are imbibing this through the effort of your waking-sleeping consciousness, so to speak (it's yet to be fully awakened), but be assured that beneath the outer shell lies a strong propensity to seek and realize the Truth of Being. You see, if you go into somebody's living room and he doesn't like the way the furniture is arranged, you can help rearrange it. But when the mental furniture of one such as you has once been rearranged according to a higher lifestyle, a divine lifestyle, it can never be put back. You cannot return to a position outgrown. So, it would behoove you to realize this before pursuing the Unfoldment in any great depth. You will never be the same personality that you now think you are if you pursue this in depth.

    A man once said to me, "Will you speak to anyone, Mr. Mills?" And I said, "Yes, if they can get here." And he said, "Oh, that's great. Well, when do we talk?" And I said, "Well, I go fishing with anyone who wants to come along, because I love to fish . . . but occasionally I catch a few flounders!"

You are treading in an area here that is absolutely, fantastically beautiful. And you never have to use LSD or any of the drugs to enjoy it. If you enter the Higher Consciousness and approach the Promised Land spoken of in the Bible, you will be consciously aware of all that transpires in and as your experience. You will come close to the Source, which may bestow its Grace by giving forth freely for a moment a sense of enlightenment or greater awareness. I don't know if you have thought deeply on this or not. I think you must have, because otherwise you could not be here.

> Dennis: Since I've gotten into this I've done a lot of reading into various topics: astronomy, mathematics, psychology, and so on, trying to answer my own questions, and wondering whether I really know myself as well as I think I do.

As you know, in building a structure of any kind, such as a structure of awareness, you have to dig deep and put everything substantial into the base, because the building can only successfully rise in proportion to the strength of the base upon which it is built. In creating the structure or superstructure, you also have the aid of a scaffold. You can build your structure with a good, solid base, and you can use your scaffold to erect the building. And then when the scaffold is removed, you have the finished work. But if there is a crack in the structure, having once built the scaffold, you know how to re-erect it in order to mend the exterior condition. And then you can take it down again.

So, the structure is of awareness and the questions and wonderings you are experiencing now can be answered for the time being via the scaffold of knowledge. But the structure of awareness will eventually carry you to an area in your consciousness that far transcends the one of knowledge. You see, knowledge is usually garnered from the storehouse of humans who walk the earth and give us these vast and interesting source books. But any knowledge can only be as valuable and as truthful as the insight of the man who recorded it, the man who "discovered" it. But if his premise wasn't accurate, neither can the knowledge in the books he wrote be accurate. And unless he works from the standpoint of his at-Onement with the Source, his so-called knowledge is more fiction than fact, because it would only be dealing with the things that are here today and gone tomorrow. But the Essence, you see, the Source, which illuminates all knowledge and all ignorance, is eternal.

So, knowledge, like the scaffold, has to be eventually dropped. You take as much from it as is good, but you have to develop a scale or a standard by which you can evaluate the knowledge. Whatever weighs in the balance you can accept; whatever doesn't you had better discard. This is why you must come to terms with Principle, with that which is fixed and immutable in your understanding, which will enable you to build the foundation of your structure. And this is why drugs are so dangerous, you see, because most of the people who take them haven't any bearings or foundation in fact. They know they can fly, but they don't know where or really how it's happening.

A man came to see me one night who had guided a great many people in Yorkville. I had heard of him and he knew of me through a mutual friend. He came and we had a very interesting time. I think he had taken LSD over one hundred times. I listened to him talk from nine until twenty past eleven and I never said a word. Finally, I couldn't stand it any longer and I said to him, "You've got to come clean; I can't follow you. One moment you're speaking absolute metaphysics, and the next moment you are speaking semi-metaphysics, and that is impossible. If you do this type of thing, you only bifurcate your experience and build on the sand."

You see, semi-metaphysics is not accurate, because it has you weighing matter and idea on the same scale, which can't be done. "Absolute metaphysics," as Mary Baker Eddy said, "exchanges the objects of sense for the ideas of Soul," but that is not an entirely accurate way of explaining it either. You must come to terms with something that can appear as a Principle in your life and as your life. Tonight you realized that one element of your life that seems quite functional and trustworthy and which can serve for the time being as a reliable foundation is your thinking capacity. But you must go still further. Albeit, thinking will lead you to that yardstick with which you can measure what you have accomplished in building your structure of awareness. If you don't develop this yardstick of thinking in accordance with Principle or absolute metaphysics, you may have your feet on the ground and your head in the stars with all these lofty considerations, but you may be falling apart in the middle without even knowing it. This is how so many people get airy-fairy about spiritual discipline in general and consequently never realize a very balanced, happy, or practical way of life.

Look at North America, for instance. We have all kinds of food for our stomachs, we have all kinds of intellectual accomplishments, but few of them have ever been elevated to the stage where they could be experienced on a higher level of consciousness, a non-verbal consciousness, the mystical.

Any mystical experience "softens" you, if you know how to interpret it. In other words, the mystical experience breaks down the adamantine intellect and enables you to intuit a life beyond the apparent level of three dimensions. But if you don't know how to interpret or view the mystical experience correctly, it can drive you mad. You may end up in an asylum! So the mystical is nothing to fool with.

To develop an alacrity in discerning fact and an ability to be unmoved by the fiction that confronts you is an achievement that few people have. Those who do have this are usually noticed, liked, and then disliked, because the others who notice it find they can't have it without paying the price. That price results in an item that is very costly: the technique whereby you have the discipline at your fingertips or in your consciousness to transcend all the fairy stories you have been fed since you started to assimilate the data coming from all the various media of today. If you don't have this technique, you may appear queer or strange to others, and you shouldn't appear this way. You should appear attractive.

The Vancouver Jester was at one of the collegiates recently, and one of my piano students was invited to hear him speak. I think he was rather loud and disturbing from the reports I got. He was asked by someone in the audience why he wore a jester's suit while lecturing. He said, "To attract the attention of the people." At this point my piano student said, "But I should think that what you know would be the attraction, so you don't need the suit!" Apparently he was quite stunned by this and by a couple of other remarks. After his lecture or performance was over, she approached him again and said, "How dare you leave this auditorium and all these people in such a state of confusion." He replied, "I'm leaving because I know you are here." Then she said, "You may know it, but no one else does." Afterwards, when people had started to leave (this part is rather delicious), a man who was travelling with the Jester came up to my student and asked, "Young lady, how did you come to this awareness?" And she said, "I have a friend," and she apparently gave him my name. He said, "Well, what does he do?" And she replied, "Well, you know, they call him a piano teacher!" Isn't that delightful? But anyway, you see the great fun I have.

You know, it's quite interesting, I go out quite a lot, but I'm seldom taken for a pianist. I'm often taken for a doctor, a lawyer, or an Indian Chief! No one really knows what I do, until they ask me point blank. And this is part of the technique. I once said to someone, "Remember, you must come to a point in your experience when you can be what anyone wants you to be while you remain centred in what you really are." It's very good, because you will then find that your experience will be richer every moment.

Very few people understand that you have to discriminate. That's why Jesus spoke in parables, because only those who had ears to hear were to be invited to the feast. But it was soon learned that even though they had ears, they didn't necessarily hear; and even though they had eyes, they didn't necessarily see. Just because someone's eyes are open doesn't mean that he is awake! So don't cast your pearls before swine, which is the unprepared thought. It takes a lot of quiet, a lot of patience, a lot of time, and a lot of great happiness to develop the technique of which I speak. Gad, I don't know what I'd do without it. I love it. And it is something that anyone can have, because everyone has already got it; they just don't know it.

Dennis: Most people are afraid of being alone with themselves.

It's nice to get rid of those "selves." Those attachments are not good because you must be free! If you don't get rid of those selves and if you don't recognize the various characters that seem to parade as you, you will become "schizo." If you are divided and don't realize it, you will have no control over which self is out at any particular time. It is the man who doesn't have control over this that ends up a wreck. It is not his consciousness that is at fault; it's the fact that there was not enough discipline somewhere along the line to enable him to know which self was out front doing the acting at any particular time, so to speak.

So, you have come to the point where you realize that the life experience so far is purely a mental one. You see, there is no reason to matter and there is no matter to reason. Without the re-evaluation of the picture you become mesmerized by it, you become one with it, and you support it and give it a reason for being something that it is not. Instead, place your allegiance, your support, and your all on That Which IS.

You are really very fortunate to be pondering this at this point in your experience. You know, there are so many just like you, but you see, not very many are really able to come to an agreement with That which launched the earth into its orbit, which would bring them into the gravitational field of those who might enhance their biped experience. You have your chance.

Has this given you any new ideas?

> Dennis: This helps ideas in the back of my mind to come out, and it just takes time.

But you see, it doesn't take time to think right! And it doesn't take age. You can't storm, you can't use storm-trooper tactics to conquer the mindfulness of Mind. It's impossible. You have to acquiesce within your Soul or within your True Nature and realize that you are a child, regardless of your years. You are a child in the programming of the Divine until you realize your at-Onement with the Divine, call it whatever you like: Light, Love, Truth. Something that may mean very little to you at this moment may be the very quality that could usher you into the Light, if you allow yourself to enter it. And that something is Love. It is so misinterpreted. It is not what you think it is at all. It's so misused.

> Dennis: Well, isn't love sort of the oneness of things?

Love is still greater than that, because it is said that "Greater love hath no man than this: that he lay down his life for his brother or for another." And the only life that can be laid down is the one based on the lie or fallacy that man is living as one of men. That kind of "men-kind" is not the kind of man that enters the realm of Light. The man who knows is not going to be fooled by the picturing and the imagining of the mind, which presents a world in which "all the men and women are merely players," as Shakespeare said. He's going to see that the world is a stage and that his Consciousness lights it all up. He's not going to be fooled and call others anything but what he himself is called, and that is "Man made in the image and likeness of the Creative Principle." There is no division. Unity, Oneness, the Aloneness of Being, is made manifest and appears on the world stage when supported by philosophical discernment, mystical fragrance, and practical activity, thus evidencing the equipoise of thought-force. That is the world that God created. So many men today feel responsible for their world. They should be *response-able*, but not to that part of themselves that tries to usurp the prerogative of Deity. Man should cleanse himself of the concept of being a creator and realize his at-Onement with the Source that launched the earth into its orbit and said, "Peace, be still."

This little bit of talking, I know you didn't expect it, but because you're you I decided I would tell you about some of these things. Perhaps this will act as a springboard. I think it has already. With your bridled enthusiasm you should arrive at a wonderful conclusion and be open to experiencing a higher level of awareness. It takes the enthusiasm and vitality of your God-Being to do this. You can read a thousand books and you may not find it. Somebody recently said to me, "My goodness, in your few words I have learned more than I did from reading half a dozen books this week!"

> Dennis: I often find myself in reverie, even while talking with people. It's become quite a concern. My mind gets so focussed on one point that often I'll have just finished a statement and find myself standing there staring and everyone staring at me. It comes as a shock every time.

Yes, this is an important area. I had somebody say something very similar to me just a week ago or so. It would behoove you to be extremely alert, because when you are carried away like that, you are carried away on a mesmeric stream that silences that part of you which acts as your director and guide. If you lose this you can create an accident both in the physical as well as in the mental realms. You see, if you don't know what you are doing on the physical plane, you won't know what you are doing on the mental plane. It tells you in Proverbs, "A word fitly spoken is like apples of gold in pictures of silver."[1] Be very alert.

---

[1] Proverbs 25:11

## Thoughts and the Divine

*Logic will never take you
into this transcendent State,
but it seems to be one of the rungs
on the ladder.*

# 2  Thoughts and the Divine

June 19, 1968, Toronto, Ontario

The question of Divinity is a profound one, and we have to be very careful with the answer, so let's see what it is. First of all, what does Divinity mean to you?

> Mel B.: I would think that a person who thought himself Divine would have to believe that he was acting on a very high and spiritual level.

The person is never Divine. Divinity conceived and spoken of by men can only be conceived when viewed from the standpoint of God, because the Divine Element is that which transcends the precariousness of being imbedded in material concepts. The Father of the idea called "Divinity" is protected and lies serene in the Unutterable. Sometimes, in an attempt to utter it, we call it the "Source" or the "Void." You see, the essence of the Word itself lies with the Source, and that is why John said that the "Word was with God and the Word was God," and thus it is immaculately conceived and exalted to the Statehood of Divinity. It is the promptings of the Divine Element, in spite of the suggestion of the personal or human sense, that impels us to pursue that mercurial feeling which is aroused by some inner aspect of our Being. Its Source is really in and as the Unutterable.

So, as man comes to a greater awareness of what he isn't, what's left over is what he IS, and with this "residue" we recognize the great gift to all mankind, that which David wanted and prayed for and that which Solomon wanted, and that is wisdom. Man in his frailty cannot presume to enhance or entrench within this orbit of Soulfulness such a thing and have it adulterated and called "human." It would soon seem to be what it is not. It would not be wisdom; it would be foolishness. So, when wisdom utters its voice, exalt it and restore it to its proper place, at One with the Father, as a result of having experienced, even unconsciously, an attunement with That which we call "Divine."

The promptings of That which is within you brings you into contact with that which seems to be like you, and it is this magnet that draws all that is rightfully yours unto you. On the spiritual level it will draw you unto that which is spiritual, and on the mundane level you will have the opportunity to be what you are, and perform and act with confidence and wisdom in what other people term the personality experience.

> Mel: I can see that. In fact, last night I got involved in a discussion on Judaism, and I argued vehemently until 3:30 a.m. At that point I said, "I must go home; I'm very tired," because I was not getting anywhere.

This is why you were tired, because you don't need to argue. You never need to argue when you know what you know, even to this degree, because you cannot convince anyone of anything. You see, when you hear something and say, "Oh, that's terrific, and I believe it" or "I agree with everything you've said," you mustn't put it outside yourself. What you think you heard and found acceptable is all because it conforms to the higher sense within you, but since you haven't heard it verbalized before, you think it's me. If you say, "I like it," it's really within you. So, it's already yours here and now, and this is something that would be well for you to store in your mental storehouse, because this is what you can draw upon. You have experienced the word on this level, and next time you will experience it perhaps on an activity level. Words without works are not the evidence of God but of the God-less. Many talk a great deal, but don't do or act. Doing has to be an attribute of the God Principle, because you can never even think of God without first thinking of man. You can't say the word "God" unless it arises in your consciousness. Your consciousness of God is the consciousness that identifies you as the thinker; this thinking thinker projects a God concept, a God idea. The Consciousness that lights this up, however, is one with the Source, and this is the evidence of it. The thinking itself is perhaps the only thing that we have on the mundane level that points in some way to the immaterial condition called God-Being. So, every time you think of God, this is your God at hand and not afar off. It's the only God you'll ever have until you come into agreement with the statement "I and my Father *are one now*," and not "shall be one." Have you understood?

> Mel: Well, not completely. I think it is largely tradition and religious upbringing combatting my logical thought processes.

Logic will never take you into this transcendent State, but it seems to be one of the rungs of the ladder. So use it, until you come to a point where you don't need it. You will arrive at a state of awareness where you can drop it. If you can't reach that state or if you do reach it and you don't seem to be able to sustain it, you can always use your logic as a step or as one of the rungs of the ladder to arrive at this level again until it becomes constant or fixed.

> Mel: Well, this is the case. There are times when I feel that I have it, but then it goes back again. I put myself through turmoil. I wish I could just solve it immediately, but after so many years it becomes ingrained into my conscious thought processes so much—

Yes, you're well-computered.

> Mel: —and I react like somebody has pressed a button.

You react instead of respond.

> Mel: That's right. This is when I find myself getting into arguments and discussions, never winning and never losing. I always seem to find myself at the point where I started.

Yes. You remind me of a car. When you turn the key and leave it in neutral, you use up all the gas but you don't make any real progress; you use up all the gas but you don't go anywhere!

> Mel: That's exactly right.

All you do is wear out the parts.

> Mel: Well, I was extremely tired after . . .

This is why you were fatigued. You got into your argument from the standpoint of trying to enlighten. You see, you can't enlighten anyone or anything. The Light is already lit! The only thing you have to do is bring it out from under the bushel.

What is transpiring in your experience is something to be watched and protected. It is such an advantageous thing to be sensitive, and you have the warmth that knows enough to protect the germination of the seed, which, like the mustard seed, can move mountains. This perhaps is why you will find, if you try to speak prematurely, that you will usually "abort," so to speak. And then you have to plant the seed again, because you didn't look after it properly.

You see, you don't seem to take the necessary precautions or exercise the proper respect for what you know is a spark from a higher level of consciousness; you don't really mother it enough. You have to nourish it, look after it, and take care of it. You don't show the seedling to your friends and say, "Isn't the bloom great?" when it hasn't even come into bud yet! And when it comes into bloom you don't have to say, "Isn't it great?" They'll say, "It's so beautiful. What is it?" It's the same thing with you. They're apt to say, "You're so marvelous. What are you and who are you? Whatever and whoever you are, I want to be that also." This becomes the magnet, the inner attraction. It becomes inner awareness and not outer persuasion.

When you argue, you are giving power to something that knows the hour, and thus could be fatigued, because you are not positioned as you should be. You must not become trapped on the plane of relativity!

## The One Activity

*If you are constantly reasoning from the standpoint of matter, you are bound by that which doesn't matter!*

# 3    The One Activity

June 26, 1968, Toronto, Ontario

Barry B.: I make friends a little easier now than I did before, so that's hopeful, because I want to make friends.

As long as you are friends with yourself, this is the most important thing, because if you can't be on friendly terms with this individuality, heaven forbid that you should be involved in friendships with other personalities, because they are never satisfying. Are you friends with yourself?

Barry: Difficult question. That's comparable to "Who am I?" actually.

I think it's better to say "What am I?" because "who" gets you involved with the programming that makes you think you are solid, and you can't go by this illusion. This is where academic teaching tends to waver, because if you reason from the standpoint that matter matters, you will never be led to the standpoint where you can "drop" your reasoning and enter a higher level of perception, which will eventually be called higher awareness. If you are constantly reasoning from the standpoint of matter, you are bound by that which doesn't matter! And that's why matter is matter, because it's limited to begin with. The only thing about you that isn't limited is that attribute that you so express now called thought-consciousness.

Barry: You prefer believing in energy?

Oh, of course. I believe in the One Energy. And I don't believe; I know. So therefore I never argue about it. You won't either. You only argue when you don't know, because when you know, there's nothing to argue! You wouldn't argue that $2 + 2 = 5$ from the standpoint of mathematics. You might from some other standpoint, but not from mathematics. If you think that $2 + 2$ could be 5, then you would always be arguing on the side of error. In order to get rid of the supposititious 5, all you have to do is come to that higher sense of consciousness called a teacher, who shows very easily that there is nothing the matter with the 2's, it was just that you didn't view them correctly. So you say, "Oh yes, I see it's 4." And you go out smiling, because you realize the correctness of the answer. What prompted you to go to your teacher? It was the erroneous concept about the 2's.

A problem arises when people, instead of seeking a qualified teacher, go to kindred people in order to try to find out what they aren't, and when you go to a level of observation and comprehension that is on the same level as your confusion, you remain in bewilderment. The only positive part about this state of bewilderment is that in the wilderness you are able to come to terms with what separates you from others. Bewilderment is like a man in no-man's-land where you find only those with you who are in like condition. But you will come eventually to some form of polarization that pulls you to one side or to the other, until your balance is established. This can only be established by laying the foundation stones that go deep into the structure of Being.

In this understanding, you can appear to be one of men, but having structured your foundation correctly, you can serve every service that is demanded of you because you know that you function on a different level, a higher level, even though what appears as you is like other men. Unless other men know the Man of them, they never recognize you for what you really are. This is it. You can always fulfill your function very simply and easily by being what you are when you are confronted by what you are not.

Have you given any fundamental thought to who you really are, what you really are, where you really are, and why you really are?

> Barry: Well, if I have, I probably really haven't recognized it. I don't think I've ever really asked myself this question — what, where, and all the w's thereafter.

You should.

> Barry: I have never been in a situation before to do so. I never really have had the background enough to do such a thing.

You could become an intellectual without the ability to see the trap, but you won't become too engrossed in this now. You can become an outstanding intellectual by not being one!

Barry: What's your definition of an intellectual?

One who is trapped by his programming and doesn't realize he's programmed.

Barry: Would you consider teaching programming?

Most teachers think they are teachers and therefore they are programmed. They *think* they are, and thus they fall into that category. In trying to tap the Higher Consciousness, which frees you from the limitations confronting what calls itself the human race, you will invariably find yourself buffeted about by human opinions, which are really worthless. People are being prompted today more than ever to get out of the mass, which always seems a mess. They are starting to walk with the liberty that is part of the declaration that man is free in his relationship with the Higher Self, which resides, to the one who thinks he needs to locate it, in the "heart cavern." So, you go there whenever you need to, until you are secure in where you Be. Then you fulfill your function of walking the earth plane with the grandeur of the royalty of your Being, which appears as the attraction.

Don't personalize it. If you do, it will be destructive. You cannot fool in this area, because you are treading on forces that you don't know about. This is why this conversation will be tempered but rewarding, kind and loving; and the way you respond will indicate the depth inherent in your higher understanding of consciousness.

With all your "w's", you have your valleys, but you also have your peaks. You see, you can go to the peaks and look down into the valley and see what is trapped; but having arrived at the peak, you know the route may have been a circuitous one; but when you get to the top, you can look down and realize that the peak of at-Onement can be attained instantaneously, and this in no way inhibits you from viewing the landscape before you. You can go down, seemingly, into the valley, but never leave the heights where you live and move and really have your Being.

You know, somebody asked if I would always talk to people, and I said yes, if they could get here. I always go fishing, but unfortunately I catch a few flounders now and then, but I don't think you're one! I want you to realize that if you pursue this Path, which is Uncontradictable (because it is the one known by its works as well as its words and by its

Spirit as well as its Soul), you can walk transfigured and with a transcendent consciousness through the various routes of this lifetime. But it is *not* to be treated lightly. The speaking that confronts you as this personality with a label can move you to change the mental framework in which you think you live, and you may not be able to put it back. You have to be very sure within yourself that you know what you want in your life experience. You are protected in the early stages of your approach to this Work in this respect: you will not be able to remember a thing that is said if you shouldn't remember, and if you should remember, you will never be able to speak it until you realize there is no one to teach and no one to tell. Then you can speak. That is the framework in which we chat.

> Barry: What if you find the "w's" unanswerable?

They are never unanswerable. You never have to be concerned about that. As long as a question arises there is always a satisfactory, provable answer. If the premise is correct, you are never in doubt.

The New Age is close upon us. It's the age of mental dexterity and flexibility, accomplished by being correctly positioned and knowing that you can never lose that position, because you are, by Divine Decree, at one with the Source, regardless of the framework in which you seem to live.

The struggling of a new idea, if it is sincere and if it has been conceived in purity and not as a fling on the mental realm, will always be taken to the delivery chamber of the Higher Consciousness. The waking consciousness, you know, is actually quite asleep. You say you are awake, but don't fool yourself; most people are asleep with their eyes open!

What you see as this [the world, etc.] has all been manufactured and presented to your consciousness because of what you really are. You don't know this at the moment. So anything that comes out of the mouth of this one that is found acceptable is really all being registered, sorted, and labelled within you, and at some point in time you will see that what confronts you as another is actually all a result of your own making, and it comes to you as the evidence of your fullness. This may not be completely discerned, but when it is fully discerned you will be completely satisfied. In a way this is what Jesus meant when He said, "Love your neighbour as yourself," but He didn't add, and I'm sure He meant it though, that all there is to your neighbour is the Self!

If somebody comes to you bearing something that you don't like, it is marvelous, because he brings it to you in order to give it up. You say, "I don't like it," and you say, "Why don't I like it?" It is because it doesn't conform to what I AM. If it doesn't conform to what I AM, it doesn't know me as I AM. So, you can say, "Peace, be still, get thee hence, because I don't know you." In this way, whatever it is that is erroneously parading can give itself up, because it lacks a sponsor.

If you need a pen, and you don't recognize what a pen is, how can you find it? If you do recognize one, you can't help but have it, because you'll always have whatever you need. You can always have what you want, always. There's not one thing under the sun that you can't have. But the unfortunate aspect is this: you may not be so glad after you once get it, because after bringing it into your experience through wanting, you also bring into your experience the work that is necessary to maintain that which was wanted. In the Divine Scheme the verdict is that it is all done and it is all good and it is rare, because it is all One with the Father of Light, with whom there is neither variableness nor turning. So you take everything to the Light, and then you see everything for what it is and for what it is not.

This approaches the very important subject called metaphysics by which, through study and practise, you come to see what IS; and by knowing what IS you see what *isn't,* or in other words, what IS is not. And knowing what IS enables you to lovingly embrace what isn't for what it really IS, because you know what IS. But you are never fooled or buffaloed into believing that what isn't (what IS is not) has any power over you, because you know what IS as you come to know what "you" is. And the connecting link is the subtlety of the IS/is. You must realize that you are the activity, the Am-ing of the I. That's why "I and my Father are One—I AM THAT I AM."

These thoughts expressed have been triggered by your Higher Consciousness whether you know it or not, because I know what I know because I know as I AM, and as I AM, there are you also. These statements must have meaning to you or you wouldn't have responded to them, and if you haven't responded to them, you haven't heard them.

> Barry: I think the question I have approached most often is "Where am I?"

Well, what did you find as an answer?

> Barry: Several answers, but none satisfactory.

Give me one. If you give me an answer then I'll have some idea where you are and perhaps where you should be.

> Barry: One was probably triggered by a desire to define time. I was trying to think of time as most likely a label for something that doesn't really exist, except in my mind, and therefore I still don't really know where I am.

No, because you don't know where you think. Thinking is only the outward manifestation of that which believes it is a thinker, but it is a marvelous tool because with it you can take it to the point where you can discover its Source, which is thought-less and yet completely thought-full. Some paths are confusing because they call it the "Void," "Nothingness," but when you arrive at the Point, you will see that it is all Thought-full, Unutterable; it is not a vacuity. So you see, when you tune what confronts you at the moment as your thinking machinery into a less-restricted subjective framework, you see that all there is to tomorrow is Now and all there is to the past is the fragrance of Now. The past, the present, and the future are all relevant to that which is able to cognize these supposititious conditions of existence on this clock of time.

Now, when you come to see who you are, you can appear to be on the clock of time, but you will move with spontaneity and enthusiasm so that no one will think you are different; but you know that what you are was never strung on time or hung up on it. The people who get hung up on time are those who think that they came into a birth and think they inevitably have to die.

There will never be a moment when you don't know that your "I" exists. The deep sleep stage is your proof of the Work [i.e., the "I" testifying to its all-encompassing nature] manifested on the level of the person, because when you arise from a state of deep sleep you say, "I slept well." That which testifies to the condition of the "I" when the little "i" with the dot (the personality) was unconscious is an indication of that Consciousness which knows not of different states of consciousness, but is forever declaring itself "I", in spite of suggested conditions of materiality.

I don't refer to "you" too much, because if I did, you might think I was speaking to you as someone outside myself. I don't want a sense of division to parade with you. But then again, if you think that all that confronts me as you is my Self, I might not say anything at all!

Barry: You needn't say anything to your Self.

That's right. But if the clarity is present, anything can be said. This is perhaps the weakness of the teachings of the Masters of India and Tibet. They realized that all that confronted them was the Self, regardless of bodies, and therefore many refused to speak. This kept so many students tied. This has come down through the annals of time. The Masters sat in silence for days and the disciples would wait for a crumb to fall from the Master's table. But it was pretty "crumby" in many cases, because all that the disciples could ever do was talk about the crumbs they got! If the Masters had seen with more compassion, they could have done what was necessary, knowing that in Divine Consciousness it was never done, because behold, it was *already* done and it was good. There is only One . . . and Man is the image and likeness of God, already complete, fulfilled, and satisfied, even if he doesn't know it now.

Somebody once said to me, "Are you a Teacher?" And I said, "Where does your question arise? Who asks the question if it isn't that which seems to need to be taught? Therefore you have what confronts you as a Teacher." But you know you aren't a "Teacher" as such, because there is no one knowing or not knowing Truth. There is only Truth knowing. It is said that Jesus went to the mountaintop, and when He was "set," in other words, established in His Christ Consciousness, His disciples came unto Him and He opened His mouth and they saw it as somebody teaching them saying, "Blessed . . . ," and you have your Beatitudes. Yet the Christ Consciousness appearing as Jesus wouldn't have seen it that way at all. I'm sure He did not think of himself as a Teacher or as one of a series.

Perhaps this will change your framework of reference, as I'm sure it has. Perhaps it will throw your computing out, which is good! But unfortunately you have precluded a breakdown in the adamantine structure of your personality, let us say, because the sharp points [i.e., of the foregoing conversation] have been dulled by your intellectualization. At a later time you may be able within yourself to use the sword of Truth and cut asunder anything that would bind you or hinder you in becoming what you really are, which was proclaimed from the beginning of time to be the Son or Manifestation of That which launched the earth into orbit and said "Peace, be still." And as John said, "These things have I spoken unto you, that ye should not be offended . . . but these things have I told you, that when the time shall come, ye may remember that I told you of them."[1]

---

[1] John 16:1, 4

Barry: What is your role, Mr. Mills?

I can fulfill many levels while being only the One activity. I never mind playing a role because I know what the Light is that illuminates the world stage, so I know the part. Until you have arrived and have stabilized in the depth of your Self, you should protect yourself. Love everyone; you don't have to say it or feel it always, but that which is like you will always be with you . . .

I know what I AM and I know what you are,
And I love what I AM and I love what you are,
So stay where you are and love where you are,
Because all there is to where you are is where I AM.
And where I AM there may you be also,
Because the "I" goes unto the Father.

*Be Still . . .*

*In the growing awareness
of right identification
will be the fulfillment
of the present incarnation.*

# 4   Be Still . . .

October 16, 1968, Toronto, Ontario

The past is nothing but a dream to the Now, and the value of any dream is in the waking up from it. So, in reviewing your past as it has been brought to your conscious attention, evaluate it in such a way that it blesses you now. In the blessing of the Nowness is the potential of the individual released, and a sense of poise, balance, and stability arises in the experience. In the growing awareness of right identification will be the fulfillment of the present incarnation.

The joy of Being who and what you are far transcends the concern and the challenge of trying to meet, through the personality channel, the commitments of the earth day. The man of God's creating walks in the Light of Day, which is the radiance of happiness and joy. There is no darkness or night in this concept of the Divine Day, which is where you live and move and have your Being.

Whenever anything contrary to this State of Beingness confronts you, ask for that suggestion's identification. If the suggestion does not belong to your inherited storehouse of Divine Life, Truth, and Love, and the glory of Being at-One with your Primal Cause, then admit it not, because it will only distress and upset you. The satanic influence that we have to contend with today is not like that of times long ago and far away, when it was supposed to have worn two horns and a pitchfork. The diabolical suggestion of today is very subtle, because it appears not external to you but calls itself a *condition* of you, and when it can relate to you by your conscious acceptance of it, the erroneous suggestion rams and pierces you. Allowing yourself to be swung among the vascillating conditions of mind and ego creates all there is to the life force of this entity called the devil. God is a word meaning "good." Therefore, if Good is all there is and none besides, where is evil going to hide?

Now, if you live from the standpoint of knowing who you are and what you are, you will transcend the process of leading a double life, and you will find the One Life manifested. Thus, you no longer have life dammed. To live in the bosom of the Father and to acknowledge Him is your freedom from being cast about in the turbulent world picture, where you seem to live and move and have your Being. You are primarily a spiritual-mental Consciousness and are only seemingly walking around with a body. The relationship that seems to exist between the spiritual-mental Consciousness and the body (they are really one) fulfills the need for those who think they need an objective sense or identity to satisfy and sustain their yearnings for the Higher Self. True, we see the body manifested, but it is really supported by the attributes of the God-Child which you really are.

Now the child on the human level is the means of maintaining the race, especially the race of family or the race of lineage. You may "suffer it to be so now,"[1] but the Child of God's creating is a little bit different. He is not a child of a day or a year; He is of eternity. The Child of God's creating is the Child of Being. Thus, when you dwell in this state, you are bearing your child in a sense of humility to the feet of the Fatherhood and Motherhood.

The problems that confront people today are of their own making. Most people love to create problems. They apparently cannot stand prosperity, peace, and tranquility. Whenever they have the time for leisure, they don't seem to know what to do with it! They go on creating and thinking a fictional world and then call it a factual one. For instance, the paper world of commerce and finance can be not only blown away and burned away, but it can also be washed away, and even more simply than that, it can be thought away. So, you arrive at what is left after the dollar sign (false sense of substance) has had its day. And you will find that the peaceful mind can come to grips with its own inherent value or substance, because in the Substance of peace, man has the opportunity of coming to the recognition of his Divinity within. It is stated in one of the great inspirational books, the Bible, "My peace I give unto you; not as the world giveth, give I unto you."[2] And the nation that cannot stand the peaceful existence pursues other levels of existence that can satisfy, within its own framework of reference, a logic of good and evil.

Individuals who cannot stand a sense of peace or stillness manufacture a sense of busy-ness and consequently never have time to light on the Tree of Life. The sense of turmoil or distress within a person is like a magnet; it draws distressful conditions to him. In the Age in which we

---

[1] Believe this to be the case for the time being.
[2] John 14:27

seem to live there is a new potential open to people like you, because of the Force that launched the earth into its orbit and said "Peace, be still." Know that I AM; I AM Mind, and as Mind, all that "I" have is thine. Claim your heritage, claim your legacy, and be still. In this stillness may you enjoy the rhythmic harmony of Being at-One with the Music of the Spheres. The Universe of Mind and of God-Man is a harmonious one in which are played, in a harmonically balanced and rhythmic way, the various themes and tunes that are easily identifiable. These "tunes," or resounding, ageless Truths, will never lose their identity in the creation of man, his church, or the universe. In this understanding of creation as it IS and not as it seems to be lies your freedom, your health, and your wealth. It's the same old story of Truth in all its glory. You and only you will write the final cadence.

## Moment of Consciousness

*Words are marvelous,
but they should lead you eventually
to the point
where there are no words.*

## 5  Moment of Consciousness

October 21, 1968, Toronto, Ontario

A conversation with Yvonne H. on the morning of October 21, 1968. Yes, Yvonne.

> Yvonne H.: Sometimes my activity is so dispersed that I feel I can't do what I must. There's no time for stillness, you know. Every minute is taken.

Well, as you know, every little moment has a meaning all its own, and this is indicative of the Divine Moment of Consciousness, which bridges over all the gaps in what appears as your activities, which you live seemingly as a person. The obligations, seemingly external to you, are being naturally fulfilled in the easiness of your loving nature. You recognize so well how your potential is being used, but the difficulty arises from the fact that in its use, you appear to experience a dissipation of the force and control that would enable you to utilize your activity so that you can let it go as a purely personal endeavour. You must recognize the impersonal and Deific Force that is omniactive in all departments of life and in the universe, in spite of man's attempt to limit, through objectification, all that transpires before the seeing of the eye.

It is well to translate and stand guard at the frontier of consciousness, always checking for the right identification and classification of that which takes place in your daily life. Never permit a moment of the impatient, frustrated sense of activity to come into your experience. If you do, you will cloud your ability to let go, you know, and let God take over, so to speak. It's not that you don't recognize this; you do. But at the moment it comes to you through your personality channel in such a way that you, as many others I know, think of yourself as a medium for the Primal Cause or Source. The concept of being a medium is the weakness in the mental structure, which could appear as the deterioration of the structure called the medium.

It is always well to realize that in spite of the suggestion of a medium, the actuality and evidence of the spiritual nature of all activity and all being is always present Now. This helps to capitulate all that you do and all that you are into an activity pattern, be it in the physical, mental, or spiritual realm. There is no division in the activity of Mind expression. But we must not think of ourselves as "expressors," as mediums, because the expressor ("reflector" or "reflection" of Truth), like the mirror, can be shattered.

You are at that point where you have within your conscious framework the promptings of your higher consciousness striving to come forth. These appear like the pricks that Job felt.

> Yvonne: I know that I'm motivated from this Inner Source. I have faith in it; it gives me strength and direction, and I'm grateful for this. I see that it's wrong, then, to worry about where I fit in, as a medium or whatever.

The worry itself would be the obstruction, and it would be the first stone in the building of the dam. The Adam man[1] is always thwarting his attempts at unfoldment, because he always feels that he is the personal builder of his experience and his world. And of course in a way he is. But if he doesn't realize his pristine heritage and divine right as Son of the King, he creates castles in the sand, which will crumble and which cannot withstand the batterings of doubt, worry, or fear. He will not recognize his awareness of the correct positioning at the focal point of the centre and circumference of Being, which is "Consciousness is fundamental, and what you are conscious of constitutes your experience" and "I and my Father are one" and not "shall be one." It's all here and now, but if you think you are hung and swung on the pendulum of time, then it's very hard to knock at the door of the eternal experience of your at-Onement with the Source.

I perceive that you have feelings of inferiority. You *feel* all the things that you know you should be naturally experiencing. You feel them rather than experience them. Feeling is fine and dandy, but it has to be exalted. The feeling nature has to be redeemed, because it also must have its source in the God-Nature, otherwise it can be perverted and adulterated. If it is, the strength of your whole spiritual awareness is for the moment held in suspension. In actuality, it is really never touched, but it is held in suspension as your real inheritance, your real legacy, until you come to realize your true identification, your acknowledgment, and your agreement to be set and established as the Child of God.

---

[1] Adam man: the archetype of the material-minded man.

Thus, the inherent capacities of your Creative Principle manifest on every level of consciousness, because "where I AM there may ye be also." The I AM, in its graciousness, appears on any level of consciousness that wishes to recognize it and has the humility to recognize it. The I AM in itself, however, transcends all levels of consciousness. It's a "suffering it to be so now" that enables that which thinks of itself as the three-dimensional human expressing divine attributes to have the I AM at hand, so to speak. But in essence It can never be brought to the borderland of the material world with the hopes of spiritualizing matter through the ability to reason. Mary Baker Eddy pointed to the idea that reason and revelation must coincide to form a new standpoint. In the revelation, or the re-evaluation of the world picture, it will be seen that the world of man has done all that it can to support that which thought itself a pilgrim on earth. The Man of God walks enthralled, One with the Father, and thus embraces the Universe of Mind as Idea, and this includes that idea that has satisfied his need called "the world."

The setting has already taken place at the right hand of the Father, and the whole picture, be it of the world or the universe, is lighted by the light of understanding, revelation, intuitive awareness, and insight. All these different levels of consciousness are there, and the One Consciousness includes all of them. It only appears in the educational process that you can separate them and say that one is this consciousness and one is that consciousness. It's only a "suffering it to be so now" until the comprehension dawns that the One Consciousness reigns supreme, and in its supremacy lies man and his universe.

There are not two creations; there is only One. The Creative Principle *is* fulfilling itself because it is bringing to birth in your awareness and in my awareness the greater awareness of That Which IS.

What else is there, Yvonne?

> Yvonne: What you've just said reminds me of a statement: "Let us all now sympathize with those who try to synthesize That Which IS with that which isn't."

That is wonderful, but as you know, sympathy, like pity, is not a good thing to have. Sympathy and pity have to do with the physical; compassion has to do with the spiritual. A man once said that pity is a ghastly entanglement.

> Yvonne: I once heard: "Love is grateful in victory and compassionate in failure."

The reason love can be compassionate in failure is that to Love there is no failure. That is why you can appear to be compassionate to that which thinks it has failed. A man who has failed has merely failed to recognize that the failure was a stepping stone on the ladder or on the path to the redeeming of the suggested failure. In the redemption will come the clarity that the failure was nothing but a progressive step misidentified. Anyone who talks on and on about failures draws more failures to himself, because he never identifies the failure as a stepping stone.

> Yvonne: It's a cumulative negative force.

It is, if left as a failure.

> Yvonne: There's a statement in the scriptures that all things work together for the good of he who loves God.

That's right.

> Yvonne: You can't fail with that philosophy.

No.

> Yvonne: So in that context there is no failure.

Correct, there isn't.

> Yvonne: Another statement: "Life is a succession of experiences rather than an accumulation of years."

Right.

> Yvonne: Here is a beautiful statement: "The body is the temple of the spirit."

That's right, but body has to be taken to a higher level because if you don't realize that "body" is something other than what it appears to be, you will fall for the belief of growing old. But when you realize that the experience called *body* is actually the embodiment of right *ideas,* then regardless of how the physical body seems to be, you are what you are. And this has nothing to do with time. So you can appear ageless, because in actuality you are!

You seem to be fulfilling a function of life on the level of the world scene, and you are doing so for reasons that are perhaps not evident to your awareness as of yet. Perhaps this earth is a stage on which you are able to fulfill with grace those unfinished activities that you have accumulated in your storehouse.[2] You will also find it possible to enhance those attributes that have until now been left in an embryonic stage. Your gestation period is coming to its fulfillment so that the Child of the Creative Impulse within you will be seeking expression on a level of performance that will meet the demands of the Nowness of the Age in which you live.

The time in which we live has been termed by some people as the "New Age" or the "Age of Aquarius." In this Age it is believed that man has the ability to walk out onto the world stage, which is lighted as never before by the inner glow of his mental fortifications, and to be supported by his Soul force in such a way that whatever needs to be done he can do to satisfy the need of all.

You know, all people are not equal. We must discriminate, and discrimination is one of the higher laws of awareness. Identification is essential, because only through right identification can you discriminate; otherwise you will judge, and we must judge no man.

Yvonne: Do you mean to say that every soul does not have an equal task in the world?

The souls, so to speak, are equal in that their Source is the same, but their evolution could appear to be different to those walking the plane embodied in three dimensions. To the Christ Consciousness, there is no difference in essence. You see, the encounters that you have with those who at the moment are unaware of their True Identity appear for them as blessings in disguise. They say, "I feel great when I am with this guy or with this gal," because they recognize, while in the presence of one who does have some degree of awareness of the Christ Consciousness, that they are able to release into expression more of what they are. They start feeling the fun of being that which they really are. And at that point will often come the "questing" time. They'll start to ask, "What is back of this thing

---

[2] Karma.

called me?" I'm sure that you yourself have been with people with whom you have felt much freer and to whom you were able to relate.

>Yvonne: Yes I have, and there are others to whom you know you never will relate. I usually sense this immediately.

Yes, I know you can, and this is good. Your sensitivity is a precious thing, but it is also a dastardly thing unless you can bring it to the point where the messages sensed do not incense you, but only alert you to the divine qualities, which should be expressed or manifested within your own consciousness as activities, words, and feelings. This in a sense is a protection, you see, but to be sensitized without a protective shield leaves you open to all the attrition and ambiguous conditions of others who might walk into your ken.

>Yvonne: And you are tossed like a leaf in the wind.

That's right.

>Yvonne: You must remain firm.

Yes, and positioned,[3] because in the positioning you know where you live, where you move, who you are, what you are, how you are ... and *Now* you are!

>Yvonne: And that you must do.

Knowing these things, the doing is inevitable. From the viewpoint of Man as the image and likeness of God, from the viewpoint of who you really are, you can scan the plane of activity, which confronts you, and you can immediately see any negativity that comes to your awareness to give itself up. It comes to you to give itself up not because it is like you, but because in coming to you, the fictitious dream no longer has a chance to parade as a reality. Consciousness is fundamental, and what you are conscious of constitutes your experience.

>Yvonne: And there is one basic Consciousness to which we are all linked.

---

[3] Practising being set in the higher state of consciousness.

The God Consciousness. You see, the one salient feature which has to be seen really for what it isn't, is that which confronts you as your objective sense (your body and your matter world). It is a making within your consciousness. You create it, but if you fall for your creation as matter, as substantial, you fall for the limited experience of matter. Matter, being limited from the beginning, can only be limited in experience and in expression. But when you see as I AM (the real Body), then you can enter this objective field and partake of it and enjoy it and see it for what it seems to be, but you know it for what it isn't.

The gods of this world are the matter gods and this is the trouble that people have. They create their own gods with feet of clay! Even the saints did this and that's why they crumbled. They personalized their understanding. Personalization, of course, can end in so many different ways, but it ultimately returns to a state of nothingness, which is dust.

> Yvonne: Words, as vehicles of understanding, must be metamorphosed and returned to the spiritual planes.

Yes, but like anything you see or hear, the word verbalized is really the clothing of a non-verbalized idea. Words are marvelous, but they should lead you eventually to the point where there are no words.

> Yvonne: Subliminal language, in other words.

Yes. This will be the communication of the future. The words that we use now are fulfilling a need until we arrive at the state of the unspoken Word. One day there will be an instantaneous recognition transcending the slowed-up use of words. As you know, words can be so misinterpreted.

> Yvonne: I recognize that and I feel that music has an intrinsic part to play in this.

It does. It is the most demanding of all the art forms and of any profession on the mundane level, because it demands cooperation, sincerity, patience, willingness, and humility to approach it with any sense of ever accomplishing.

> Yvonne: Do you feel that my pursuit in understanding all the musical techniques of composition is vital and useful and in some way fits in?

It does. It enables you to tune in more accurately to the Pitch of your real nature. You at the moment are perhaps a bit out of tune with the stabilized vibration of your Being, but of course it is the sensitivity of the inner hearing that is prompting the outer listener to come closer to the Pitch of true Being.

Now, this is only being portrayed on the stage of the world where every man and every woman is "merely a player." Your sensitivity of hearing with the inner ear will take you to a higher level of consciousness where you will vibrate in a harmony intrinsic with your innate vibration and thus find the concommitant expression on this level of comprehension. And it will be recognized by those who vibrate in harmony with it. When there is dissonance, see it for what it isn't and let it go; when there is concord, claim it for what it is because here is the harmony. Within the set triad of Being[4] is the unification of That Which IS, and with the division and the separation of the triad, there must be the resolution. It is done from the standpoint that God and man are inseparable. It is the Primal Cause being voiced to the material world which says, "This is my beloved Son or Self in whom I am well pleased." This is the only critique that man ever faces and this is the only judgment that can be passed upon man.

> Yvonne: And thus will the cosmic evolution be carried out.

It is already carried out. It is only through our limited seeing that we see it in stages.

> Yvonne: "He that hath an ear let him hear."

Yes. You can see how fortunate you are, because you have another one too, another ear.

> Yvonne: Another ear . . . the inner ear.

Yes, this is your sensitization, which can wrack you as well as enrapture you.

> Yvonne: Until you bring everything into harmony.

Well yes, until you walk enraptured.

---

[4] Life, Truth, and Love.

Yvonne: And is this ecstasy?

This is the divine condition. It is only man who claims it as an ephemeral and spasmodic condition, an "ecstasy experience." It isn't. It's permanent, continuous.

Yvonne: It's the state of Being.

It's the state of Being unconditioned by the mind of man.

Yvonne: After which we strain and yearn.

It's only a straining and yearning after That which in essence already IS, either you wouldn't be bothered straining and yearning after it! It is only the prompting of the inner Self that makes you go on. You see, you feel dissatisfied because somewhere in your consciousness lies the sense of satisfaction. Within your framework of reference there must be the sense of satisfaction already present and realized, either you couldn't appear dissatisfied. And it's the same with unhappiness. In essence you must have happiness, either you couldn't think you were unhappy!

Yvonne: I have another statement that I wondered if you would comment on: "It seems as though sometimes you are precariously perched above the earth and the slightest puff could blow you back into that murky maelstrom."

That's true as long as you think as person instead of as God. You see, you can't ride two things at once.

Yvonne: Yes, I was going to say that's a sign of duality.

Yes. You mustn't fall for the illusion that it's "you" who are growing in awareness. It can appear that way and be exciting and everything else, but the work that has unfolded here this morning has been done universally. It has been done not just for you or for the world, because that would be limiting it. It has been done for the entire universe. "Universe" means "to turn into one." Everything that is happening has to be carried right to the Oneness. Don't personalize anything; just let it be.

Yvonne: It's interesting, you know, in retrospect, to remember how I've prayed through the years. For a long time it was that I might serve God, then that I might know His Will, and now that I might become one with Him.

That's very beautiful. What you've said is so apropos, because the Aquarian Age is considered the Age of Cooperative Service. The word "prayer" comes from an Aramaic root meaning "adjustment." When you pray you are really being brought into adjustment with the Law of Being. So you have prayed that the law of your being may be brought into adjustment for cooperative service. I would think that even at this time you are fulfilling your prayerful wish; your actions verify this. From here on your experience will be more and more a clarification of your at-Onement with the Primal Cause, which you are so readily aware of.

## Identity and Individuality

*Don't be too satisfied
with being this personality;
become the Individual you are
in the image and likeness
of the Creative Cause.*

# 6   Identity and Individuality

October 29, 1968, Toronto, Ontario

When the personality or the little "i" testifies to its condition upon awakening, we so seldom recognize that it is really testifying to that Source which gives it life. Consequently, people fulfill the day experience, unless they *do* wake up, in living a fantasy life, because they believe that that which confronts them [i.e., the world] is real and substantial. But that which is substantial, of course, is incapable of deterioration, incapable of annihilation, incapable of any destruction whatsoever, because that which is truly substantial arises side by side with the "I".[1]

It has often been said that you are the world you wander through. But you see, when your days of meandering become wearisome, your thoughts may then turn in a direction that will lead you Home. Not satisfied with wandering, the thoughts must come to a place of rest. The fact that has to be considered is where and how this picture called man and his world arises.

When man born of woman enters upon the earth stage, he is taught to identify, through the senses, all that confronts him. Through the years he comes to accept the sense testimony as factual, and thus is left in a state of distress when there is no unity in the sense-responsive framework that has been built up through his education. When one prompted by his higher Self starts to question the substantiality of his matter world, because it exists through the senses and the language that has been built around the senses, he arrives at a state whereby he almost loses his identity, because with the eventual annihilation of his senses [i.e., death] he wonders where he fits into the picture. Yet the senses, being confined to the matter object, cannot really tell an accurate story at all, because premised on matter and belief, they do nothing but build conceptual castles on the sands. Matter

---

[1] From the standpoint of That Which IS, the world is no longer seen in its illusory (changing) aspect, but is seen as being not separate from Reality. Hence, the world, as it really is, "arises side by side with the I." This paragraph touches upon the paradox of the world being both real and unreal—all depending on the state of consciousness of the one perceiving it.

has to be seen for what it is, just as the body has to be seen for what it is, and man has to be seen for what he is. Now, the idea of body is one that is terribly important, because you seem to walk with it and you seem to talk with it, but what is it? How do you identify it? How do you feel about body?

> Bill M.: I am aware of the fact that I am something considerably more than body. My meditation tells me that, when I lose the sense of body.

With the arisal of the idea of body comes also the arisal of that awareness which identifies the idea and carries the idea in mind. Mind always evidences itself as consciousness. That's why we say that Consciousness is fundamental, because as long as you are conscious you will always be embodied; you will always have that body which is necessary for you at the time you seem to need it. It will be one that will fulfill its function for you wherever you seem to be. At this moment it seems to be as it confronts you [i.e., material], because it is fulfilling the demands of your Soul.

> Bill: Why am I not conscious of this? Why must I be caught up in the body if I am aware that I have it for this purpose?

You will come to see that you are caught in it because you tried to usurp a prerogative of Deity, and you tried, perhaps even unconsciously, to put the little "i" with the dot on the throne.[2] But that cannot stand. You can never put the greater into the lesser. So, you are perhaps caught in the trap, the seeming trap of duality. The feeling of humility must ever come to the consciousness for acceptance in the Soul's reference for feeling the Being I AM. On the material level, you prove to your own questioning sense the fact that you exist by declaring "I am," little realizing that it points to "I AM That I AM."[3] The feeling of Being I AM is the Soul of I AM, which is all wrapped up in the rhythmical pulsation of the Heart I AM.

---

[2] Referring to the error of identifying the Self with the body-ego consciousness.

[3] The reason one does not perceive "I am" as being associated with "I AM That I AM" is that one associates with thoughts, and "I AM That I AM" is not a thought. Upon reflection, one realizes that he already is the I AM identity without even having to think about it.

The duality picture does not in any way affect the fact that the Unitary Principle underlies reality. The One can appear to be expressed in multitudinous ways, but there is no division; there is only the One. Regardless of a thousand men, there is only one Man. And that which knows "I AM" is all there is to man. The one who does not realize this is one in a mass, and one in a mass is always in a mess! That's why you stand apart, because you innately know that the Father of you is the God of you, and that which recognizes this is Christ Consciousness.

Don't be too satisfied with being this personality; become the Individual you are in the image and likeness of the Creative Cause. Creative Principle fulfills itself. You must obtain the freedom of being what you are, because if you don't know *what* you are, you'll never come to know *who* you are, *where* you are, or *how* you live and move and have your Being.

What poses itself, Bill, to your sense? Would you like to say anything? I'd like to know where you are.

> Bill: I think I understand that everything that comes to me is idea, but I can't seem to go any further than that. There's something blocking...

Well, that's because you think it's *my* idea. If you can accept and understand it as *your* idea, then you won't put it into my lap. If you do, you see, you keep it outside yourself. That is why it is very important for you to talk a bit, because then you might put your foot in it! You are idea, Bill. And when you meditate, you should always establish yourself as the impersonal viewer, because you might otherwise become trapped by the mind's picturing and fall for an erroneous identity.

> Bill: Occasionally, I have had glimpses of the fact that I am literally nothing but consciousness. As I look at you, I recognize that you are an idea, but somehow you are more than that, namely, that you have consciousness as well.

Yes, the idea and its corresponding identity always go hand in hand. You don't talk about God; you talk about God and man, or you talk about father and son, or mother and daughter, or knife and fork. You always think in terms of the compound idea.

Bill: Well, I am able to see this sometimes, but I am not able to hold it. What must be done in order to reach the point of knowing at all times, and of being able to keep in consciousness the awareness of the consciousness?

You will be able to hold it when there has been an evaluation and a re-evaluation of your experience from the standpoint of revelation, because revelation is nothing but the revealing or the re-evaluation of the world picture. It doesn't take time to think right, and you are really not hung on the clock of time. The idea of you trying to maintain the higher awareness is just the reason you don't. You don't have to support awareness; awareness supports you. Awareness becomes yours with the price tag of recognition. The recognition of awareness is what prolongs awareness, but the moment you start to try to hang on to it, you lose it. So, as soon as you struggle to maintain your awareness, you've already lost it. Acknowledge it, recognize it, and enjoy it. Awareness will eventually become the springboard to insight, and when you have arrived at insight, you can't explain it, no matter how hard you try.

Insight is just another sound, but it leads to a higher level of awareness. It is a name that helps the mind to understand. It's like the trinity of consciousness, for instance, that people speak of: the material, mental, and spiritual levels, which are names invented purely for educational purposes. Most people become confused with such concepts, however, because they fail to realize that they really can't divide Consciousness. These concepts are only meant to help you separate the chaff from the wheat, so to speak, to help you to evaluate your various experiences. The important part lies in always remaining unified in your standpoint when engaging in this sifting process. Let all the kernels fall, see them for what they aren't, and always go back to the fact that Consciousness is fundamental.

It is of interest to note that each of the three levels of consciousness can be broken down still further, each one can have its own divisions. Each one can be divided into its own trinity. For instance, the highest level of consciousness, the spiritual level, consists of the trinity of understanding, intuition, and insight. Awareness, via intuition, passes into the higher state of insight, all due to being triggered by understanding. Understanding is father to it all. Similarly, on the thought or mental level, you have the trinity of thinking, the intellect, and the mystical.[4] You seem to start out as a thinker thinking thoughts, but if you are fortunate, you become familiar with the mystical, the unspoken feeling world, which both entices and transcends the intellectual computering. When you have once become satiated with the results garnered from thought activity such as this, there arises a sense of dissatisfaction. Then you realize that the intellect must be elevated, and this is done through what is termed metaphysics. Via metaphysics, the mystical may be activated through a resultant intuitive grace.

At this point one must be alert to prevent any break or division. Thinking coupled purely with the metaphysical-intellectual is cold and abstract, and the results are usually impractical. Similarly, the metaphysical-intellectual, coupled with the mystical, without the activity [i.e., active, enlightened participation in worldly affairs] is also impractical. It becomes the pastime of dreamers, hermits, and beggars. This has been the trouble with India. However, in the balanced trinity, you have the thinking supported by the metaphysical-intellectual-mystical, bringing into balanced expression a motivation and an activity recognized by man as that of a higher, spiritual calibre.

Always remember that consciousness can't be divided. When you have arrived at the point of insight, which is one of the highest aspects of the higher consciousness, you will find that you have your metaphysical-spiritual-intellectual and your insight walking hand in hand with what some people call Cosmic Consciousness. When all this is brought into proper focus and you see the undivided garment of the Whole, you may realize that you have walked into Christ Consciousness.

> Bill: Does Cosmic Consciousness happen through thinking or does it literally just happen?

It happens, and then you know that what you thought was a thinker thinking thoughts all tied up in knots is superfluous!

> Bill: Can it be induced, or does it just happen? Can it be approached as . . .

It can be approached, but only in humility. You can't storm it, you can't force it, and you can't will it, because it is the Legacy of the Father

---

[4] *Thinking* in this case refers to the creative aspect of the mind; *intellect* refers to the mechanical aspect.

of Light with whom there is neither variableness nor shadow of turning. Unless you claim your Legacy and your Inheritance, which is rightfully yours because of who you really are, you cannot "walk enraptured like some holy thing."

As one person said, "The trouble anyone has is in believing he is the physical nobody which he isn't, instead of appreciating the spiritual somebody that he really is." We think we left Heaven for earth, when actually that state of Consciousness is here and now, and it includes the earth in a blessing, takes the world in its arms, and embraces the universe. The world doesn't owe you anything, but the universe does. "Universe," when traced to its root, means "to turn into one." The world, on the other hand, is the fragmented, dualistic concept of creation. It "aborted" in the mind of the human.[5]

Bill: Can you sense why I am having such difficulty in understanding Oneness?

You are thinking of Oneness as something that is going to happen; but it's because it has already happened and IS that you are here. You are projecting it into a time sequence; but there is only One Event, and that is Now. There will never be more Allness than there is right at this moment.

Bill: I sense that what you are saying is right, but I can't really feel it.

Well, it doesn't necessarily have to be felt. It is the acknowledgment of it that is primary. Through your acknowledgment you open a door and let the sun shine in. You have kept many of your inner windows closed to the brightness of That which you really are, because you haven't accepted what you are on the physical plane. Thus, you are finding it very hard to accept what you are on the spiritual plane. That which you are on the spiritual plane is much more difficult to accept in a sense, because you really haven't evaluated what you think you are correctly. You always tend to evaluate yourself from the standpoint of what you have been taught to believe is you.

---

[5] "World" originates from the Indo-European root "wiros," which means "man; life or age of man; men together." Thus the contrast is seen: from the standpoint of the universe, man is seen as a Unity, the manifestation of a single, solitary Consciousness (God). From the standpoint of the world, man is seen as being divided; several billion individuated, material beings.

But you see, when you come to evaluate the landscape, for instance, especially your own conscious landscape, you can't do it by being lost in the trees, so to speak. You can't be. Always take into consideration those little upright stakes upon which you get tied and stuck, in other words, your thoughts. You have to leave the thinking as a thought that would trap you. Go to the place from which you can view the vista that lies before you. You know, if you climb a mountain or fly in a plane and look down upon the earth, my goodness, you then see how deceiving the whole picture was while you were down there on the surface. It's all a matter of observation.

> Bill: I'm beginning to get the feeling of what you're talking about.

If you can just ride the rhythm of what is being said, you will start to feel the impulse and you will start to feel the meaning. It's just like a piece you play on the piano. If I just played notes 1, 2, 3, 1, 2, 3, you wouldn't recognize "God Save the Queen." It is only when there is a rhythmical flow that the melodic line starts to take shape. It's only when the rhythmic impulse is felt that the form starts to take shape.

> Bill: Previously, it seemed to me that reincarnation made a great deal of sense, but with the new concepts that I am now getting, it doesn't make any sense at all!

It is not so much what you have been, it's what you are *now* that is important. Then you are able to see what you might have been, but you won't be a has-been!

> Bill: All of that makes no sense to me any longer, and that sort of destroys one of the basic premises I accepted.

Tell me, when you came to realize that there truly wasn't a Santa Claus, did it spoil the fun of the holiday? It just went onto a different level. You accepted the fun of the holiday and everything that went with it, but you did so on a different level. Your level of observation changed, but you could play the role of Santa Claus if you wanted to. And if called upon, you were still able to fulfill the wish of the child who still believed in Santa Claus.

> Bill: If we all share the same Consciousness, how is it that some are aware of this and others are not?

It is just like five or six people in a car driving down a road. They all have their eyes open, but very few people see the silver cup lying beside the road. I often observe this with people. We are all conscious, but what we are conscious of constitutes our experience.

> Bill: But how can my experience be separate from yours?

Because you are what you are by the law of your being, just as I am what I am by the law of mine. The one thing that we have in common is Beingness, the activity of Being the "Am-ing" of the "I". The Am-ing points to activity. You never just say "I"; you always say "I am." "I am Bill," "I am hungry," "I am satisfied," or "I am healthy, wealthy, and wise." Reference is always made to the I and the Am-ing.

> Bill: This means that there are some parts of consciousness that are aware of themselves and others that obviously are not.

People, you see, seem to believe that *they* have consciousness and do with it as *they* will, and that's why some appear to be unconscious and why some appear to be awake. But when you have awakened in That likeness, which you really are, then you realize that the limited consciousness was only sustaining the thought until it awakened to the Fact that is All. In the theatre you may play the part of Hamlet and fulfill all the demands of the Hamlet experience, but it is fascinating that when the lights go up, the Hamlet personality fades, and you realized all along that your real name and individuality was fixed and untouched. So, the big thing is to remain what you are when you are confronted by what you are not. This again raises the idea of identity, which concerned you so much last night. Last night I talked about the rod of identification and passing under it, and how the correct identifying process brings with it a sense of being reborn. The old man must be put off. It's a second birth, you see.

> Bill: Well, again, you're very perceptive. I feel I have a reluctance to let go of individuality.

You'll never let go of that.

Bill: I'm not certain I follow.

Your personality is certainly limited, but your Individuality[6] is limitless. When you realize the Individual you really are, the personality that people recognize as Bill will be pretty staggering! I can tell you now that as this awareness grows and becomes part of your conscious activity, you will have to be very, very careful. You will be like a bright light, and moths will always go to the bright light. Don't personalize it, because everyone else will. They will tell you how wonderful you are and how much they love you, but always toss it right back into their laps by acknowledging the Source of all beauty and all perception. This is great fun, no matter who says it.

The New Man is a balanced individual in all areas of life, and interestingly enough, it is the area of male-female balance that perplexes you. The balanced condition of male-female polarities that you experience is not understood by your personality. It comes to me that this is also one of the reasons that you have put on a kind of armour, or heavy coat of "mail." You don't really need it. Instead, the soft and delicate inner nature, which is the female aspect of you, must be recognized and brought forth in your consciousness and no longer buried beneath your personality's censorship. This inner recognition will become the shield and buckler to the personality as a result of the power and the magnitude of the tenderness of the Love that really is you. For some reason it has been buried in you.[7]

Bill: Yes, you're right.

If I permitted myself to take it in, I would feel sadness. But this is really a joy, because this is your gestation period. You are truly pregnant. The ideas discussed have been planted and they will bring forth their fruits when the vine can sustain them.

---

[6] Indivisible Nature.

[7] On the male-female polarities: "The female is a conscious state identifying primarily with the conceptive, intuitive, and nurturing nature. The male is a conscious state evidencing authority, virility, and vision. When these qualities are united with the female qualities, you have a conscious state evidencing the conceptive, intuitive, and nurturing nature with authority, virility, and vision." (From an Unfoldment given on August 11, 1978.)

Bill: Then presumably it's up to me, on the conscious level, to make certain the vine grows strong as rapidly as possible.

Yes, and then be as unconscious of it as possible. Just put your roots deep into the soil of a New Earth so that the branches may reach to a New Heaven, because in this awareness, the old heaven and old earth must pass away. It has always been said that you must bury the old man, even if he's twenty-one or sixteen! The New Man of the New Age is quite a different creature. And you are one of them.

Bill: You sense this, do you?

I'm positive of it. I don't think you have any alternative; some people do, but you don't. You will be treading a unique path because of your own uniqueness. But your path won't be like anyone else's; it's impossible. You see, you must relax in knowing that your unfoldment will not necessarily occur because of you; it will occur in spite of you. At the moment you think it's in your hands, and it isn't.

Bill: Yes, yes, you're right, I do.

But it isn't. And it has slipped more out of them this evening than you'll know. There has been much going on tonight that will bear fruit in a short time. The soil is fertile and the seeds have been planted, but they're infinitesimal at the moment.

Bill: You have been very perceptive about my basic characteristics. I certainly hope you are right in this regard.

I'm positive of it. You needn't have any concern whatsoever. I can hardly wait to see the changes that you will evidence in the days to come.

Bill: Do you think that there will be the release of that block you were referring to?

Oh yes, completely. It won't stay around for very long, because tonight, in this Day, this Radiance, in this Effulgence of Light Consciousness, the deep hidden recesses have been penetrated. A room can be closed for twenty years to the light of the sun, but all you have to do is open the door and it is immediately filled with light. And no one will ever know that there was darkness there. It's the same with you. You must have patience.

> Bill: Yes, I agree, but patience is certainly not a virtue of mine!

You have a lot of patience, Bill, but you just don't know it. It is your frustration with yourself that you experience as your impatience. You get very tense in your solar plexus area because of the lack of patience.

> Bill: Yes, I do.

You see, the plan of man has nothing to do with wanting, wishing, or desiring. Desire is often at the root of impatience. Unfortunately, desire and prayer also go together in people's consciousnesses and attitudes. Desire after righteousness is one thing, but it can become pretty fevered. Look at the Crusades, for instance. The same warring goes on today, but on a different level, in a different way, because we are living in a different Age. It is an Age where all these suggestions, which confronted man in bygone days as the outward movements of masses, are being instigated into destructive activity on the lower levels of consciousness. Unless man is alert to this, you see, he doesn't realize that he may not be thinking his own thoughts. He may instead be going along with suggestions. In the old days, they used hocus-pocus and mesmerism in order to destroy. The aggressive forces today are having the same effect, but on a much subtler level. It's happening in the realm of consciousness, which is far more serious.

> Bill: Are the aggressive forces themselves part of the One?

In essence they are, but in appearance they are not. The One lights up all of creation, good or bad. Take the sex urge, the sex drive, for instance. Sex is part of the power of the Creative Force, but usually remains unredeemed.[8] When redeemed, however, it becomes the fire, the Kundalini fire, which has great spiritual significance. This is very important. All of man's attributes must be redeemed. Their redemption draweth nigh, because we are walking and living in an Age where the powers of the mental realm have never been so exposed or so easily appropriated. This is why

---

[8] That is, seldom thought of beyond the limits of the physical plane.

the church is having its day, you see. It's not meeting it, not at all. When you come to see what you are, then you may appear to go to church if you want to, but the point is, when you come to realize that *you* are all there is to church, then you can go or not go! And you can do or not do . . . but you cannot Be or not Be.

> Bill: Humility is something that I don't really think I understand. If we are the One and One is All, then why should we necessarily be humble? If it is a God-Force, then is humility a suitable attitude toward it?

Humility enables one to lay "me" down and relax. Without it, you see, there is tension and pain, because your search becomes a burden. Humility is that which enables you to say, "Not my will, but Thine be done." You see, the last will and testament of your Father says, "This is my beloved Son in whom I am well pleased." He is the only Critic who ever spoke about you as you really are! But if you try personally to usurp that Wisdom and that Divine prerogative, which only comes to you via the right of Sonship, you are treading in a precipitous area. You will find yourself having to characterize an attitude that is uncomfortable and live a material role that is not at all suitable to you. It's too heavy. It gets so heavy on your shoulders, because that Divine prerogative isn't really "yours" in that way.

> Bill: The question is, how is it shed?

Oh, it is shed! As I said earlier this evening, it doesn't take time to think right! I'm sure this false sense of personalization will be gone this instant. It takes no time at all. You just expect—someone once said, "Man exists at the standpoint of expectancy."

> Bill: I'm sure expectant, but I can't seem to understand the concept you brought up tonight regarding everything existing now.

It is only because you don't believe this that you put everything into the future. This is what time does. A great metaphysician once said to me, "Time is that which would attempt to limit and to divide and prevent all the good from happening in the Now." But *Now* is the time in which the God-Man lives and moves and has Being!

## Riding the Beam

*My thanks are offered
for being able to punctuate
this mundane experiment
with celestial potential
for those men and women
who would strive to wear the Star
of rejoicing.*

# 7  Riding the Beam

November 5, 1971, Toronto, Ontario

This is the evening of November 5, 1971,

And alone we sit and ponder the questions that will arise
When the Happening of Being fills the skies,
And man may ask, "What does the face tell?"
When the day of darkness has passed and the
    shimmering starlight does dwell
As a beacon in the thoughts of mankind,
There is the joy of knowing that in spite of all the seeming,
    there is nothing but Sun-Ray, Sun-shine.

In the Light, may it come to be seen what is required, in the pattern of Unfoldment, of the Spoken Word, which may enable the dream to be seen and Reality to stand revealed. May the Consciousness of Being, alone in the Light of Love, be the prompter and the prompting to the questions that will come. May the answers and the questions be realized as one in Source. Questions and answers are all part and parcel of the human and his beliefs. The answered question points the way to the Place beyond the stars located in the Kingdom of Light—the Source of joy, comfort—the knowing All.

So, Priscilla does use her pen to take the notes, the sounds, as they flow, and she will offer some questions that she says within her arose. May they blossom from the bud-dom called "question."

> Priscilla C.: Is there a certain "beam" that one can travel on that will take one back to one's "planet," one's source?[1]

---

[1] Referring to the terminology of certain trance mediums who use planetary symbology to describe the inner nature of the consciousness of the one having the reading. A planet or star is ascribed to each person, which represents the trance medium's perception of the inner tendencies and qualities latent within his psyche. Mr. Mills stands firm in declaring that Truth needs no medium to be experienced, which the trance experience seems to suggest is necessary.

Before you attempt to trace back on this so-called "beam," find first where the beam began, where it arose. When you find out where the beam began, you will find yourself one with the Source of the beam, which is all there is to you.[2] That is how you can appear to be a beaming self. That is why all selves should beam! I have often said that you can't appear like a sad sack and call yourself the Christ. If there isn't any joy, or any surface ripple of happiness, why, anyone who comes in contact with you would wonder how far the Dove had descended upon your consciousness! The Dove must light and It always appears as the Light that chases away all darkness and gloom. There mustn't be any doubts as to man's Spiritual Nature or his Divinity.

You see, there is only Consciousness. When you identify with the body, you feel you want to have it around, and you feel you need a "beam" to ride. When you move into the state of realization of the Consciousness that IS, you realize there is no place to go or ride to. What you are conscious of is your conscious experience within and without . . . a material body.

This is the only true way to see everyone who comes into your life experience. They are lighted by Consciousness, by the conscious Light. And you see, this includes everyone and everything. This knowing enables you to appear to have a friend, for instance, while realizing on another level that the experience of the friend arises because you are conscious of what you know constitutes a conscious friend. This is what constitutes everything that seems to be experienced "outside." When you dwell in that realization, you also come to see that what you experience as love arises within your consciousness. That is where it is experienced. In the Light there is no separation, regardless of the appearance.

When you partake of a meal, you know that *you* are the tastiness to the dish. But you still enjoy your food, despite knowing that it is primarily an inner conscious experience. You don't go without it, because you still have the body around, your vehicle. It is somewhat the same with what you call your beloved friend or your friend of love. You don't try to do without him any more than you try to do without food. You know that even though the food is within your consciousness, it still appears to satisfy. Similarly, your friend is in your consciousness, and he also appears to satisfy.

---

[2] Ask to whom arises the thought of a beam. Find the source of the thinker who says there is a beam.

Priscilla: Then you would always have the friend, wouldn't you?

Yes, if it is right that he should be your friend. It is right if it is a genuine experience of oneness.

Priscilla: What if it appears that you have very few friends? What is loneliness?

View from the Absolute, then see if there is any loneliness. You have to see it this way, or there would be no way to live with your loneliness. Otherwise you will be like a lost star instead of like a Lone Star State—very rich, very wealthy, and able to supply tremendous dividends to those who would make the effort to dig into it, into the State of Oneness, the Lone, Love One, the Love-One-Star, the Star of the Love One.

Priscilla: So, if you don't seem to have many friends, you have to take care of what appears as the picture.

Take care of it, and do the work. It is how we lead our lives that is the important thing.

Priscilla: Is the word the "ship" that can take you back to the Source?

I don't know if it would be the word that would take you back. Words are like the power to your ship of consciousness and can enhance your thought field in such a way that you might find yourself effortlessly taken to the Source.

Priscilla: What would be the ship, then?

Consciousness. But you have to have the words as the fuel to guide your consciousness. You might say that the words are the fuel to your thought action. You are trying to get to it intellectually.

Priscilla: How do you move from the intellectual plane to the living experience?

You don't.

Priscilla: What do you do?

Stop bifurcating an action of mind and remain conscious. Then you won't label an aspect "intellect." Remain aware and let others call you the possessor of an intellect, and so wise. The key is to be able to testify in an effortless way to being conscious and yet to still fulfill society's model of a high state of accomplishment in the framework of being an intellectual. The interesting part is that when the society member comes to know you as you really are, he will find that he can no longer call you an intellectual. He starts to acknowledge your awareness. And he won't say you have such an "intellectual awareness." He will just say, "May I sit and chat with you a while? You have such an awareness and seem so wise." And you say, "Of course, because I always tell the elect to go in." You must be able to intellectually seemingly meet the need while remaining apart from the need and apart from the suggestion that it is something external to your Self. All is included in the awareness program of the All, even the blade of grass and the lily of the field.

> Priscilla: After you had gone to see the opera, *Die Walkyrie*, you said that as you watched it, you had the awareness that you were the Light to the opera. Is that how you also see the world, that you are the Light to your experience of the world?

All the scenes, entrances, and exits of the opera are controlled in accordance with the Composer's plan. The actors and actresses, in realizing the grandeur of the opera, wouldn't presume to say, "We will make our entrances and our exits when we want to." When they have once auditioned for their parts and have accepted them, they have to follow the script. It's the same with the world experience, although so seldom do men and women follow or even recognize the Script.

Jesus left a beautiful example to be followed. The example to be followed here is that man should follow his own inner awareness as it dawns. That is all that is being asked. Kenneth Mills seems to be asked to talk and to answer questions and to entertain, but what is the purpose of this if it isn't a transforming power in the lives of the students? They, like iron filings, should find it only natural to become aligned within the radius of a magnetic field. How easy it is for you to experience the power of a magnetic field, the magnet, and the iron filings, instead of just reading about it in a book.

When iron filings are put onto a piece of paper, they align themselves to the field of force of any magnet that may be placed underneath. Even though the magnet is unseen, the filings indicate its presence. The book may point to the fact that this is an experiment that could be conducted by men and women if they doubted the power of the magnetic field. Once men and women had experienced the experiment, however, they would know the power and would then only use the book and its pointings as a guide for any student who wishes to approach the centre and circumference of Beingness. The man who has such a goal and is willing to follow such purposeful intentions may find born unto him in this experiment an awareness of a Power that he, in his humility, may recognize as Christ the Lord.[3] It may come unto him as the descent of dew distilled by the risen fire of Love when the atmosphere [i.e., mental attitude] is ready to yield to distillation [i.e., purification]. The Promise fulfilled is not seen with the eyes. It is an invisible happening when the temperature is raised and the atmosphere that is laden with water reaches a point of releasement, which results as the dew on your rose.[4]

I am very grateful that through a scientific analogy could come such a clear pointing of the needle appearing on the compass of the Consciousness that man calls his Immaterial Power, which can direct him via intuitive promptings to an impersonal alignment with the Force Field of undetermined Might, Power, and Glory. My thanks are offered for being able to punctuate this mundane experiment with celestial potential for those men and women who would strive to wear the Star of rejoicing. That Star will appear and point to that Place where your Light will start to glow. This will appear as a light to your nation.

It is imperative that each man or "filing" becomes a magnet in his own right. Otherwise he will appear to have no purpose but to be tossed about on the time sheets of the world, whereupon someone may say, "Oh let him go, he doesn't mean a thing; he is not worth the time or the effort. He has no direction or purpose save that which is earthy, and that's bound to be dust. I want to live eternally, so I will not waste my time associating with another who has no more polarization to That Which IS than I do in my ignorance. My purpose in life is to have attained a goal whereby I know the path I wish to tread in order that my aim may be accomplished."

---

[3] The "experiment" for the spiritual aspirant consists of aligning all his thoughts (iron filings) with Principle (the Magnet).

[4] The Promise (Realization) is "invisible" in the sense that it is fulfilled beyond the mind's perception.

What is the value of men filing past one another on the streets of time, in the offices of buildings, wearing the suits of an executive and bearing no impress of knowing the Divine at work in the appearance of the diversified fields of action? No wonder there is no wonder surrounding a man who, with his beer, watches an idiot box to pass away the time, as goals are chalked upon the scoreboard as man chases a puck, or chases a ball flown off a bat or kicked by a foot. No wonder this Age of destiny seems to be one of indolence, the Age of indolence and apathy!

As we sit together this evening, it seems that we are pondering that which is happening and that which has already happened in what mankind calls the future. Do you need another pen, Priscilla?

Priscilla: Yes, thank you.

It is a trying experience when your "ship" has a limited supply of ink, or in other words, a limited supply of a marking material that would be left as the evidence that your impersonal action moved in this time, in this Age, in this Light, and in this action, all due to the Rhythm of Being and its loving embrace. You might say that this is how your "ship" [i.e., incarnation] appeared. Your wake of rejoicing has appeared as the tracings of a pen, which has left its mark as the Impulses from the celestial heights have descended, so it seems, to the level where an earth man might realize that a Force exists that can take him out of a body of weight and into the Body of Light. Thus is he able to don the garment of the Christened Consciousness and is able to come and go at the beck and call of Love, Will, and circumstance.

Yes, scribe, what next?

Priscilla: If the so-called "brain factor" results in the belief of thinking, what is the factor that results in the belief of dreaming?

The thing to do is to come to the dreamless State. Thinking and dreaming arise from the same factor [i.e., mentality]. That factor is a fraction, and there is no possible way to solve the riddle from within the riddle, when the whole purpose is to enter the State that is dreamless. Then you will find That ... a fact.

Priscilla: How do I know I love?

You don't know you love? "You" don't love. You couldn't, because "you" is darkness, and Love is Light.

"You" is darkness and Love is Light,
That's your question and there is no plight.
I answer no more a question such as this,
Because it would seem to be from just an ordinary miss.[5]
But when you know ... then U.C.[6] beams a Light,
And you no longer dream your dreams; you say, "I know the power of the Light;
It dispels the illusion that there ever was night."

That is Love.

> Priscilla: You once made a statement: "If you don't see it for what it isn't, you haven't expressed Love."

That is right. You know, I was talking to this young girl today while she was here for her lesson. She is sixteen years old and she came for her second piano lesson with me. She told me that she couldn't believe in God. I said, "That's all right, but why?" She replied, "Well, I don't believe what everyone says about God being in man's image, you know, like an old man." And I said, "Heavens, I'm glad you don't believe in that kind of God, because I don't either!" She then just beamed. She continued by saying, "Does this mean that you're God and I'm God?" And I said, "No, a person isn't God, but the Light that enables you to call me a person and yourself a person and to see another person is the evidence that there is a Power, a Principle, which man calls God." She nodded and said, "I see that." And I said, "Good. Then you can see how God could be called 'Light,' because when you say, 'I see,' it means that there is no darkness." This is something that I don't believe most people realize. When they say, "I see," they are really declaring and acknowledging the ability of the God Power to dispel the illusion of darkness.

---

[5] Slight annoyance here, because this question arose from someone who should have known better, especially after the initial remarks made at the beginning of this Unfoldment on asking questions.

[6] Universal Consciousness.

## *Only One Consciousness*

*The difference
between your mind and my mind
is the belief that Consciousness
could be divided.*

# 8     Only One Consciousness

January 18, 1973, Toronto, Ontario

> Eugene M.: What is the link between the individual mind and the Universal Mind?

Consciousness with a capital "C". It isn't *your* idea of consciousness. You see, the idea that there is a link between the Universal Mind and the individual mind is, of course, a belief. There is no such link. It is only in the realm of delusion that man thinks there is the necessity for a link. When he has realized his at-Onement with the Source, he realizes that there is no need for the belief of a link, because there is no believer to believe in the belief of a link, because there is no consciousness that is separated from itself. So, that embraces the belief of a believer until the belief fades out and the believer is realized to have only been an imposter trying to usurp the throne or prerogative of Deity.

> Eugene: What, then, is the difference between my mind and your mind?

The difference between your mind and my mind is the suggestion that Consciousness could be divided. Man has had the belief resident within his consciousness that he is a consciousness separate from another consciousness. There is only One Consciousness, which is incapable of divisibility. The grace of That Which IS enables man to appear to be what he isn't [i.e., seemingly divided] until he realizes what he truly IS in the image and likeness of the Son.

> Eugene: Does the effort to direct the thought of another person express a subtle form of personalizing?

Yes, it does, because the suggestion that you are going to influence the thought of another person is why you have no power. The idea of one personal power influencing another power that is personal nullifies what might otherwise be a renewing experience. When you speak to others, don't speak to them from the standpoint of trying to enlighten or change their thought. Speak to them from the standpoint that they have presented themselves to your consciousness to give up any sense of misunderstanding about That Which IS. This misunderstanding comes to your awareness so that it can fade out. You see, if they ask you, you can tell them; if they don't, it's better to be quiet. Don't try to instill in others the awareness of how they should be thinking, unless they ask you to guide them. It's better just to be silent and know the Truth, because it is the Truth that sets man free, not a man believing that he knows it.

> Eugene: Not the opinion of it.

No.

> Eugene: This leads to my next question: What is teaching, without trying to direct thought?

Teaching is only the name that is used to signify the happening when two or more are gathered together with the hopes of becoming one in the awareness of That Which IS. When two or more are gathered together in the presence of the One Altogether Lovely, that awareness of the One Altogether Lovely dispels the gloomy illusion of two gathered together to be taught. In the attention that is given to the One Principle Altogether Perfect, the suggestion of two being taught fades out. The adoration of the One Happening embraces what appears as the pupil and the teacher, and the two are graced in being able to say, "I know that I am so and so, until He comes whose right it is to restore my name upon the Scroll of Knowingness." One can then say, "The grace of God has been redeemed in my consciousness, and it is seen and experienced as the knowingness of my Indivisible Nature, One with the Fount of All Being."

> Eugene: Wow! I don't know if I could ever go back to the classroom again!

It's an incredible situation, because when you have those confronting you who come to be taught, the teacher would know that the teaching that seems to take place is only done as a "suffering it to be so now," until man realizes that what he is becoming aware of is his Divine Inheritance. In that recognition, the teacher fades out as a personal teacher and appears as the impersonal Principle as action. Got that?

> Eugene: It's a thought I'm going to have to work with.

Do, because the idea that the teacher is there to perform a miracle in teaching, in passing on information, is only how it appears. What actually is happening is that the suggestion of a person needing to be enlightened by the rays of the Sun is being cast away. Shadows are created only by those who would stand in their own Light. When the shadow fades, you see, what appears as the teacher and the one waiting to be taught are embraced in Light that is One. There is no shadow cast, no divisibility present, and Man Indivisible walks One with his Maker.

I think you have seen a great deal in a short time, because it is your right. It is every man's right, but not every man is prepared. I think you are. All that you see is rightfully yours, because it is your inheritance. It is not because you are particularly bright; it is because the brightness of the Sun/Son shines in spite of the shadow of person.

Eugene: Thank you for acknowledging that.

Many men and women today don't want to become aware, because they want to go on having escape routes. But there is no escape route from the truth of knowing that two and two is four. Mathematically, you can never presume it to be five. If you do, you suffer the consequences. So, you can never presume to work with Principle spasmodically. If Principle were a spasm, then man would be a spastic! And Man isn't. Man is the rhythmic pulsation of an energy field that is commensurate with the Power That IS. That Power, in an attempt to be known, may be called "Love."

Eugene: I have one more question. How do I know when I'm in a trance?

You are in a trance when you react to Love's statement of Man's wakeful condition. You are in a trance when you do not hear it. Any non-responsiveness to Truth, to Love's statement, is the evidence that you are entranced. To not recognize the Truth of such a statement is the evidence of trance. It's right there in a nutshell. The way to check the trance state is to respond to the true statement about your Self as you really are. If there is no response, then you know that you are mesmerized by personal suggestions. You see, the greatest trance state is the one that has man involved in thinking his own thoughts and thinking they are commensurate with his being a spiritual person.

## *The Quest of Questioning*

*In the knowingness
of That Which IS,
there is no question that is not
Self-answered,
and there is no Self-answer
but the One Quest fulfilled.*

# 9  The Quest of Questioning

April 24, 1973, Toronto, Ontario

> Yogi Vinod: In one human birth, how much can one be conscious of meeting the Ideal or anything one is searching for?

In one human birth, a state of consciousness of degrees is a limited beginning. From the standpoint in which this Work unfolds, the human birth is limitation to begin with. The consciousness attributed to a human birth is a limited consciousness. The point of the Quest is to free the thinker from the beliefs surrounding a human birth and a limited consciousness so that he may engage the Consciousness which will free him from being a thinker thinking thoughts, and which will untie the knot that binds him. So, if you look at this question from the standpoint of one human birth, it's impossible to consider meeting the Ideal. The human birth itself is so limited. That's why you must not fall for its appearance.

> Yogi Vinod: Would you say, then, that one passes through several lives to attain to that full awareness?

One appears to pass through the different levels of lives to satisfy the thought of those who are moving in a rhythm of lives, births, and deaths. In the awareness of That Which IS, the seeming gap that man experiences between what he calls "lifetimes" is bridged. Man sees that what appears as different lifetimes is merely the One Life unfolding, fulfilling the needs of those who would see it pass.

> Chris H.: Does everybody have those needs?

Yes, but not everybody knows how those needs are ultimately met. A person's lack of happiness, joy, and satisfaction is often a guide pointing to his satisfied state, to the state where these needs are transcended. If you are satisfied with what you seem to be, then your satisfaction is limited, conditional. But few are satisfied with what they seem to be, and that is why they constantly move hither and yon. The least speck of happiness points to the State That IS, which may seem garmented in happiness.

> Chris: So there really isn't any false happiness?

No, there isn't false happiness; there is only limited happiness.

> Anna P. H.: And you know it by its faltering.

That's right. You see, if it were perfect happiness, it would be constant and you wouldn't need or expect to see the verification of it. Thus, *you* might appear as the verification of it to those who would demand to see it while you were involuntarily fulfilling the action of the happiness called the Self.

> Yogi Vinod: What would you say is the perfect concentration?

What would I say is the perfect concentration? To listen, and upon listening, to find your Self, and others may call it a "Tone." Thinking is noise to a thinker, but noiseless to the Tone That IS. Listen. Perfect concentration also could be thought of in this way: to concentrate implies the need of one to come to attention, yet *One* should be the focus of attention! Since the One is perfect tension, when called upon to sound, It may give forth a word of meaning.

> Anna: The concentration would be acknowledgment of the tension.

That is right. Only a person concentrates.

> Yogi Vinod: Will conscious concentration bring about the unfoldment of the Self?

It will point to the Self and you will appear to be conscious, and another may say "in concentration." They will call it power.

> Yogi Vinod: Concentration is power?

Concentration could appear as power, the evidence of the Self that is All Power. To think "you" have to concentrate in order to be That which you are is a self-imposed belief. Some have called That State the "Sound of the Silence." Someone once said to me, "I will thank you in the Silence." And I said, "You may think that you have heard words, but how do you know the words aren't the Silence?"

> Yogi Vinod: Who does all this work? This thinking, concentrating, knowing, being consciously aware, and meeting, who does that?

The spurious suggestion that man is individualized and personified. When man falls for the individualization and personification of an action that is impersonal, he receives the impression that he is doing the thinking, the acting, and the living. When he wakes up, he finds that he can still appear to live and think and act, but it is all an involuntary happening.

> Yogi Vinod: What is the Source of that involuntary happening?

The Constancy that supports man, the world, and the appearance. Mary Baker Eddy once said, "The Divine Principle of the universe must interpret the universe."[1] This is the only premise from which the universe can be understood. It's a beautiful statement.

> Jaan K.: Mr. Mills, when the suggestion of a thinker fades out, do the thought patterns seem to change?

When the thought patterns of a thinker fade out, find out what thought there is to sustain a pattern.

> Anna: So a thought is only born from a thinker.

Yes, it's like the great, great grandchild. It's not that you deny thought; you only deny thought as being something that it isn't. You must come to the point of embracing thought for what it truly is. It's not denial, it's all-inclusiveness.

---

[1] Mary Baker Eddy, *Science and Health with Key to the Scriptures* (Boston: Trustees of the Will of M. B. Eddy, 1875), p. 272.

Jaan: Can what a thought truly is be defined?

In the terms of That Which IS, it can be swallowed up and defined as All, but *you* find it. Then *you* will be the One Thought, and you will name it; I can't. I'm just calling it a thought.

Yogi Vinod: How would you differentiate between the two minds, the one who is asking and the one who is replying?

It's part of the play. The play appears as if consciousness could be divided and as if questions could be asked and answers given. In the knowingness of That Which IS, there is no question that is not Self-answered, and there is no Self-answer but the One Quest fulfilled. So, it is the conscious garment of knowingness that embraces what appears to be the actors on the stage of appearance, until they awaken to the knowingness of That Which IS. There is no division. If there were, you would seem a stranger to me.

Yogi Vinod: When you say "you," it means what?

You? Take these two candles, for instance. I can refer to this pink candle or to this mauve candle, but I am only referring to the appearance, not to the body called wax.

Yogi Vinod: What is the appearance of the body?

Appearance suggests a body, and that appears as you and me fulfilling what appears as the picturebook parade. But the Body That IS [i.e., Consciousness] is a Divine Idea. As man incorporates and appropriates into his experience all the ideas commensurate with his Ideal, he will find that the Body That IS enables the body that seems to be to be light and to be called. Some will call it a candle, and some will call it ... [K. G. M. shrugs his shoulders.]

Yogi Vinod: So the one who is replying, is he really the knowledge of the knowing One?

Knowing that One is All enables the plea of a question to be fulfilled by an answer. One is All and All is One. The knowledge and the knowing are swallowed up in the Known. There's no division.

> Yogi Vinod: What is the closest way that you can express to another human being the One which is living?

By loving, and that is the power that enables one to be freed from believing he is a thinker. You see, to Love there is no thought. Love is the Power that is *Life's Omnipotent Verities Eternal.* When experienced it appears as the Power that can translate an imperfect thought pattern into a more perfected one — a metamorphosis. Right where man seems to be stands That Which IS unrecognized.

> Chris: How do you get past the trap of words?

By knowing that the word is not a trap. The word is not a trap when it is used in the service of altruism, because you wouldn't utter a word that would not be commensurate with your Ideal. The Ideal, of course, is assumed to be That which is attributable to Perfect Principle. Principle is That which is undeviating and incapable of any form of discord or disintegration. The Ideal is an image of great power. It would be well to see what your imagination has done *to* you so that you can now see what it can do *for* you.

> Chris: Being, to me, is . . .

The best way to cope with that is to find out how to get rid of the suggested "me."

> Chris: Otherwise one might think that the words come from . . .

Well, I don't think of the words as words. I think of them not at all. You might say that I never take thought for a thought. I never know what will be said, but you will find that all my words are attributable to an Ideal Principle Perfect One. What you are saying sounds so acceptable to you, but if you could analyze what you are saying from a point outside your "me," you would find that words spoken indiscriminately are only another way that the intellect has of sustaining itself.

> Yogi Vinod: Which religion on this plane at this time is the most mystical?

It may not have a name, but it could be called "the one that is birthed by one who sincerely wishes to be swallowed up in the experience of ultimate freedom." He would grasp at that experience for support until that moment arrives when, with the tool of metaphysics and philosophical discernment, the mystical experience is translated into a power of permanency, which enables the mystic to become, for what appears as others, one capable of pointing to the State That IS. The aroma and the fragrance of the mystic is a garment worn by the fragrance of Being to draw man to the Heart of the Flower. You will then find that the mystical is swallowed up in the glory of That Which IS and becomes a permanent living experience, Self-perpetuated, Self-sustained. Of the various mystical experiences that I've had, it has been this very factor of metaphysics that has sustained them. Via the awareness of metaphysics, they have been translated from an impermanent occurrence to a permanent awareness.

> Yogi Vinod: But isn't it still the mind which contemplates what we call permanency?

Just as the idea of light on this plane has a corresponding identity called a candle, That Which IS fixed also has a corresponding identity called permanency. The mind fixes it as such. But the one in that experience would be "mindless," so to speak. You know this.

> Yogi Vinod: But the mind is . . .

A tool.

> Yogi Vinod: A beautiful tool . . .

Absolutely.

> Yogi Vinod: To bring about . . .

The mind is under the Throne Power of That Which IS the Almighty One. It is never annihilated; it must be freed. What is it, Anna?

> Anna: I'm thinking. I'd like to get a statement from you as to a practical way to freedom.

Well, man is free-born; it's only the beliefs about his birth that limit his freedom. To be free, try to remember. The most practical way to be free is by trying to remember when you were born. Then you will find, and others will say you are free. There will never be a moment that you can remember when you didn't exist. But it's the mesmeric suggestion of going to bed, getting up, seeing day and seeing night that makes you think you aren't free. The world seems to be going around in circles, just like men, but not like Man.

Yogi Vinod: I'd like to share with you something more.

Yes.

Yogi Vinod: With thanks to you, I am able to see many things. I, being from the East, am a student of the Eastern mystical knowledge and now find myself in the West among the Western society. You know the West and the Western mind. Unfortunately, I've seen much poverty in the East. Due to this poverty, very few people in the East today are able to accept the Eastern mystical knowledge, and even fewer can put the knowledge into practice and unfold it.

Yet, the same thing is happening in the West. Here there is a poverty of mind. The Western mind, materialistic, loves to intellectualize everything. The Western man wants to know Reality through the mind and intellect, which basically is a wrong approach. They are incapable of engaging Reality by that approach. There is really no mind and no intellect. By clinging to knowledge, there is no way they can get to know Reality. There is no way.

The Eastern people have the knowledge in the form of ancient mystical sayings. The knowledge exists there, and it will keep on existing for centuries together. It will not finish at all. The people are acquiring more material knowledge, going into the material world, which I consider to be good, but they, unlike Westerners, have something in them which has been given to them by right of birth, and that is an ability to unfold spiritually if they try sincerely.

The Western people make efforts, but they are unable to go beyond mind and intellect. It keeps pulling them back. It is one thing for them to understand Reality with mind and intellect, but there is no way as of yet for them to go beyond it. This is so perhaps because they are far less capable than the Eastern people of going beyond their personal individual selves, their egos. In the East a person can directly look and see if someone is talking just from the level of mind or intellect. But there are few who really speak for Reality's sake, or who come to know the Reality and nothing else.

Yes, so many people don't want to wake up from the dream, and if they do, they still want to keep track of what they dreamed. In so doing, however, they still remain in the dream. If you dream that you are going to Bombay from Toronto to meet a group of friends there and then you suddenly decide that you are going to wake up, you don't say, "I can't wake up until my friends wake up, either I'll leave them in Bombay." When you wake up, where are your friends? They were in your dream, but you didn't stop from waking up just because they were in Bombay. Yet, it is so strange, when you wake up you always think that you wake up with a body, instead of seeing what the body really is. Then, you may appear to sleep and wake up, but you realize your "I" never sleeps.

You know, the idea of looseness has never been commensurate with the soundingness within me. It's not right at all. Tension is so important, because unless there is the tension, there can be no pitch of accuracy. It's like the piano. The strings have to be brought under the correct amount of tension for the piano to function as a harmonious whole. If there is one string out of tune and it's struck, there is discord. An element of discord results, all due to the lack of tension. In the West you will see much of what is called "freedom of expression." It's not freedom at all, it's looseness. You perhaps have noticed this yourself already. How long have you been in Canada?

> Yogi Vinod: About nine months.

Yes, I'm sure you have noticed this among the people here. They talk of their freedom, and yet they are prisoners of looseness. If you speak to them, they seldom give back a voice-pitch that is accurate. You know, you can walk into a room and appear to be just like any other man or woman, but your "tension" sounds whether you open your mouth or not. And others are usually aware of it. They pick it up.

> Jaan: How does one drop the suggestion of being a thinker?

Well, ask yourself who asked the question and you'll drop it mighty fast, because you have no proof of who asked it from the standpoint of a thinker! A thinker identifies himself with the body, and the body is what?

Salt, water, chalk, protoplasm, or slime
And you never saw it do anything in time.

It only outlines space. Your thought isn't in the body; your thought is *about* the body. But because you identify your thought with the body, it becomes a thought of limitation and not an idea of freedom. You see, an idea is not figured, until you demand to see its identity, and then it might appear as a candle or as a body, but the *idea* isn't the body as matter. The Idea Body IS.

> Jaan: Is a rose real only in the idea of its beauty?

The word "real" refers to only that which can stand the test of permanency. Therefore, the rose is only real as idea. But since the rose is real as idea, you may appear to have a rose and love it.

> Jaan: Is it the idea that gives the rose its meaning, which enables us to seemingly identify with it and call it a rose?

No. What gives the idea a meaning is the belief that it has to be identified. The identification lies within the idea itself. That's where it has meaning, and that is how it is limitless. When brought into objectification it is limited, just like the body.

> Jaan: From the standpoint of Reality, you wouldn't see a rose as a rose, but you would see the rose as an idea of beauty.

Yes, you could say it that way; but then it could also appear as a rose. An idea of beauty may appear as a rose or it may appear as the yogi. It may appear as you. But if we put it in either of you, then it would be limited, and you would be putting God in matter, and that's Pantheism.[2]

> Jaan: What would be calling the idea of beauty a rose?

A thinker. But you see, when you have that in its proper place, you can appear to be a thinker and utter all kinds of words, but to the Self which is All, not a word has been said. Only the Silence is heard.

> Yogi Vinod: In the East, one usually goes to learn this Path from a yogi, a mystic, or a saint. But the yogi, mystic, or saint often does not "teach" him anything. Not at all. He just gives the disciple a very simple word as a mantrum and says, "You keep on washing dishes for ten years. Do this simple work, cutting wood and bringing it to me." The Teacher often does not speak to him at all, nor does the student have the courage to ask him any questions.

This is very interesting. Someone asked on Saturday night something about questions. Whenever I think of questions, I go to that knowing Point which says that a question only arises because the Quest has been personalized. This gives you the "i-o-n." Whenever you have the "i-o-n" you know there is personalization. Whenever you have the "i-o-n," you have the materialization, you have the manifestation, the idolization, and then you have religion. You have contamination and sensation. You have nation, and then nation against nation and a world divided, because you think "you" feel. You think you have to have the manifestation, and

---

[2] The doctrine that the entire universe is God, or a manifestation of God, thus the erroneous association of God with matter or God *in* matter.

that is the demonstrat*ion*, which fails today.³ You see, no matter what you can do physically, unless it is taken to the Throne of Power [i.e., the I AM], which enables it to be done, it is deterioration. So, remember (don't do that!). Then you would have yourself personalizing the act of remembering, which has resulted in a "Commemoration Day"!

If there is a question, know that it comes because the one who is asking it is ready to die. Actually, any question that you ask should always be commensurate with the state that would free you from being a liar about your Self.

>    Neal D.: It seems so important to be willing to die to the question and to be awake to the answer.

Yes, very few people are ever aware of the answer. They ask a question, but very few are ever aware of the answer. If the question is really answered and the answer is really heard . . .

>    Jaan: . . . where is the questioner and where is the answerer?

So, this is the evening of April 24, 1973,
And we have sat in the joy of knowing the Light that
    eternally Be's.
In the recognition of All that is at hand,
May man look in, look out, look up, look down, and see
    only a Visitation, as is planned.

The Traveller of Glory appears from out the sky
That wears the garment of devotion, for man must surely die
In the joy of being liberated, in the Light of knowing that
The joy of being One is truly the legacy of man as That.

Enjoy the bliss of Being in the rhapsody of a song,
And may your heart be in rhythm, as your head feels the
    strong
Directive power of action, as Life unfolds as planned;

---

³ "Demonstration" refers not only to the political and racial issues of the day, but also to the erroneous belief that one's perception of Truth and accomplishment in Realization can only be verified by acts of healing or by miracles.

In the involuntary Power may man view the joy attributed
    to Man
Garmented in the conscious knowing "I AM That I AM."

So, those present in the company of the avant-garde of Light,
Be clothed in the majesty of beauty; have you seen a
    miraculous sight?
Look within the tulip and look within the flame;
Do you see a rose? They call it by that name.
"Before ye call, I will answer," and thus it's happened
    as 'tis planned;
When man listens, lo and behold, there is a soundingness,
    and man says, "I heard, I listened, I AM!"

## Franciscan Interlude

*The Christ contemplated
is the Christ forestalled.
The Christ greeted
is the Christ ever at hand.*

## 10     Franciscan Interlude

September 6, 1973, Toronto, Ontario

       This is the evening of September 6, 1973, in company with Joseph S. As we sit and chat here in Toronto

> It is twenty to nine
> And we will have a short visit until I find
> What it is that must be known.

       If you have questions, they should be asked. I pray that the answers will be acceptable in the sight of the Light. The one question I want first to ask you is whether or not you are finding your ponderings pointing to Self-realization, or are you finding them merely enhancing the course of natural events? The Divine Event is Self-realization; the natural event points to the unfolding streams of time, which in essence is not separate from the Self.

       What you become aware of as a result of hearing this Unfoldment must be very carefully nurtured within your consciousness. Ask yourself how and why your questions are being asked, because after you hear the answers, you will no longer be found at the same point in consciousness again. If your questions are asked for the glorification of person, they are of no consequence whatsoever. Understand me.

       We have gathered together in the power of that Frequency that man says sponsors the Way to the freedom of the Light action on behalf of those who love.

> What are some of your questions that have been prompted
>     by your heart?
> May your mind never show you anything but the Rhythm,
>     and man must start
> To ever move in the rhapsody of an unfolding pattern of
>     Light,
> Ever caught in the tide of those events that sweep away
>     the clouds that would veil the Light.

When man would see a message written in a frequency of Life, may the Glory be ever available to free him from the planet where there is the blending and the bending, but never the ending, because man will go on reaping after his own kind, until he is freed from beliefs and the giant blender called earth.[1]

> Joseph S.: Mr. Mills, would you please say something that I could remember when I celebrate the Eucharist? In other words, how can the Eucharist become a more knowable happening?

A question of the first order. The Eucharist becomes a more knowable experience by knowing how it is that man rejoices in his Unity under the auspices of Life, Truth, and Love; Spirit, Mind, and Soul; growth, seedtime, and harvest. It is then that man fulfills the Law, and according to the Will shall it be done when man gives birth to the celebration of the Feast.

In the preparatory stages of enabling you to celebrate Mass on behalf of the Self, may it be realized that in the celebration, man calls to remembrance on a symbolic level the peregrinations of the thought world as it has moved about from day to day and year to year in search of an Event commensurate with the Promise of Eternal Life. When you take a sip of the wine, you will know you have supped.[2] Because you have wandered, you will know that it is said unto you, "Stay and rest awhile, the day is far filled; won't you stay and rest awhile and sup with me as the sun sets, promising the sunrise as man walks in the light of knowing that what man is conscious of points to the Conscious Man that is to be Self-elevated as a result of the service of the bread, the water, and the wine." It would be expedient under the jurisdiction of this select council[3] that you move into a pattern where the symbols are found elevated, soaring on wings of thought as *your* consciousness is dwarfed and the Consciousness that is commensu-

---

[1] The earth as a giant blender refers to the earth as a place in which are mixed all the ingredients of human experience as man attempts to live life successfully and harmoniously, to develop a "smooth" life experience. Fortunately, Life is not a pâté made up of unsuccessful livers!

[2] Supped: partaken of the Substance (Bread) of Truth. Wine symbolizes Divine Inspiration.

[3] Those present in the room.

rate with the Self is found the inspirational happening when man is found caught in the embrace of Love. The Eucharist is a happening of transcendent Power.

> Joseph: Perhaps my next question will dovetail with the first one.

I'm sure it will. The bird is flying around this night![4]

> Joseph: What must I do to contemplate the Christ? What colour would best prepare my consciousness?

The colour of humility. The Christ contemplated is the Christ forestalled. The Christ greeted is the Christ ever at hand to bear the greeting, "Well done, thou good and faithful servant; inherit the Kingdom of Light." To prepare to contemplate the Christ is to still the thought as the C [i.e., the Christ] arises as the sun upon the horizon of a New Age.

> Joseph: The order I belong to is the Franciscan Friars of the at-Onement, the atonement.

The at-Onement, or the atonement, is the celebration that is offered symbolically upon the altar of earth as the Eleventh Commandment[5] is fulfilled in the Light of the Dove.

> Joseph: Since I spent so much time with the Sufis in California, I'm wondering what is the pattern of my being there, and how does the Christ relate to the Sufi teaching?

The Christ relates to the Sufi teaching as to all teachings as being the result of the Christ Consciousness realized. Any teaching that bears the mark of approval commensurate with Truth, Life, and Love lived relates to the Christ. The Spirit that has been called the Christ, which has

---

[4] The Dove symbolizes the ascent and descent of Christ Consciousness.

[5] Mr. Mills has regarded God's statement to Moses and the people in Exodus 20:24, "An altar of earth thou shalt make unto me ...," as the Eleventh Commandment. Earth being an altar signifies its consecration in the Light of Realization. It is also the altar of sacrifice of actions and service to God (the Self).

seemingly been adulterated by being claimed a personal possession,[6] is really the descent of that State of Consciousness in which it is realized that there is no *person* to realize what it is to have passed beyond merely contemplating *about* something and experiencing *in* voluntarily the thing contemplated about.

Sufis dance, Sufis embrace a language and a teaching that give the exercise necessary to the thought world (which is so ephemeral) so that it can point the way to that Day when man can see that there arises upon the periphery of observation That Power that will wipe away all tears from man's eyes. He will see that the valley has been lighted and the mountaintop stands, and Sufis may dance and embrace the Christ. Man claims the Christ to be the transcendent Power of the knowing action of the Law and the Will, fulfilled according to the decree of man's Ideal in the Image of the Divine. These are rare statements in a rare setting.

Joseph: Yes, they indeed are. There's one thing, the Sufis have the teaching that there is a Teacher of the Age. Who is the Teacher of the Age?

The Teacher of the Age is self-recognized.

Joseph: In what sense can I invoke or anyone invoke Divine Ideas?

Most immediately by dying to the suggestion that "you" have any!

Joseph: Is there any true synthesis?

From the standpoint of the Light that IS, you might call the only true synthesis the garment of the One. One may be garmented, in the realm in which man is striving, as "synthesis." The thesis and the *anti*-thesis, or the antithesis, results when man cannot find synthesis.[7] The Ray of Synthesis is a ray that unifies not by trying to join together, but unifies as a result of the inevitable Divine Coincidence.[8]

---

[6] That is, exclusively possessed by Jesus, or any person.

[7] "Thesis and anti-thesis" denotes duality, the world of opposites.

[8] The human and the Divine fade out in the conscious realization of That Which IS.

Joseph: How can I not make responsibility a burden?

Responsibility is a burden to one who is trying to be responsible. Cease trying to be responsible. *Be.* Where is the burden?

Joseph: Thank you. What place does the body and the five avenues of the senses have in the Light of the Christ? What is the error of sense consciousness?

The error of sense consciousness arises in the consciousness that is not freed from the belief of a sense experiencer. To the Christ there is no error, and to the Christ, that which is called error is really Truth misidentified. The error of the sense world lies in the limited consciousness of a sense man waiting to find the Consciousness One.

Joseph: What is the proper use of the body?

Embodiment as Divine Idea.

Joseph: How is the grace of Christ experienced so that I may discriminate between what is truly food and what is toxic?

Discriminate by knowing that the only food that is acceptable to the Christ is what the Christ would find acceptable as food. [Note the development of the Eucharist idea.] All else would fall into the realm of error or toxic suggestions. All suggestions are toxic, and that is why the Christ stands in that position where error can fade out in the Light of Knowingness, because to Knowingness there is no error to fade out. Often, men and women will attempt to defy such a stand, in order to evade their own responsibility, by declaring, "Such arrogance!" Of course, what appears as my so-called arrogance is only the assurance or conviction that the Christ lives in the experience of "I".

Joseph: What is the difference between spontaneous fantasy activity and real insight?

There is no relationship. Fantasy is imagination; real insight is hoped for. Imagination and relationships are both different aspects of a dreamer. Divine insight would appear when the dreamer leaves his dream state and awakens to the rising Light.

> Joseph: What is the truth to healing?
> Can someone be healed without
> acknowledgment?

Oh yes. What is the truth to healing? There is nothing to heal in the Light of Truth. Acknowledgment of the Source sustains the healing until the one healed heels to the Line of Power commensurate with the Divine State, which is, "Be ye therefore perfect even as your Father in Heaven is perfect."[9]  That is divine healing.

> Joseph: Thank you. Would you say something about the prayer of St. Francis, "Make me a channel of Thy peace"? In what sense are we channels? *Are* we channels?

In the sense of St. Francis, every man was a channel, and he hoped that everyone would be a channel of peace. In the channel of suggestion every man has to be a channel of peace, and that is why man is falling to pieces. There is no channel to Light; Light is the Power that is called a channel when limited by person or when experienced at rare moments. Light is eternal and constant.

> Joseph: How can you sin against Heaven and earth? What is sin?

You can't sin against Heaven and earth, but the reason you might stand convicted on the field of action is that you have believed yourself capable of sinning against Heaven and earth. As a believer, you inevitably carry the sin. A believer is always the sin. The sin of a believer is completely freed in the authentic celebration of Mass, because there is no such thing as a belief. The believer is only a suggestion until man is freed from the giant blender of earth, where all is chopped up into pieces with the hopes of coming out a purée! But all the chopping up and all the putting together will never put man together again.

> Humpty Dumpty sat on a wall,
> Humpty Dumpty had a great fall
> All because he thought he could do
> And didn't acknowledge the Power of All.

---

[9] Matthew 5:48.

> Humpty Dumpty had a fall
> Only because Adam bawled
> And cried for Eve, and said, "What's split my side?"
> And Humpty Dumpty jumped onto the wall,
>     and there he abides.

Man never fell in the Light of Truth.[10]

    Joseph: Thank you. What is the difference between Spirit, Soul, Mind, and Body?

They are different facets of the One Power. They are the four-square of Being: Spirit, Mind, Soul, and Body. This symbology may stir up your thoughts in the blender a little bit, and hopefully you will not come out as a purée of soup, but pure in the awareness of how all is fitly joined together in the crystal clearness of the Allness commensurate with the Divine Light. You see, Body [i.e., Consciousness] is really what we are celebrating when we are thinking, Body is really what we are celebrating when we are praying, and Body is really what we are acknowledging when we celebrate Communion as the Totality of Being. It is the Spirit [i.e., of Truth] that sets man free. The Spirit enables man to see himself as the Image with no fantasy, because in the Light of That which is real, you will find that you are in that Age where the "I" and the "AM" are fixed.

    Joseph: How can I pray for someone?

By dying to the belief that there is someone to pray for. In that moment of realization there will be the Balance, and the Balance says, "I AM All, and there is no one but the One Altogether Lovely."

    Joseph: Why can't the Buddha be called the Christ?

The Buddha *can* be called the Christ. It is only ignorance that would prevent Him from being called the Christ. They are of the same School. When people don't call the Buddha the Christ, it is because they think of the Buddha as a person. The Buddha isn't a person. "Buddha" is a frequency around the soundingness [i.e., Teachings] of Gautama. Similarly, "Christ" is a frequency around the soundingness [i.e., Teachings] of Jesus.[11]

---

[10] Man in Fact is not bifurcated, despite belief or appearance.

Jesus and Gautama were brothers. They were only separated by a few centuries of belief. Gautama revealed certain facets of the Face and Jesus revealed other facets of the Face. Now, the full Face must be faceted and faced in the Light of the Aquarian Age.

> Joseph: The psychologists talk a lot about dreams. What is the message of our dreams and how can they be used in the Work?

Well, people talk about dreams in order to fill up their dream. It would be better if the dreamer could awaken to the sound of a bell that has a pitch commensurate with never having slept. In this way, his dreams might be answered. You see, to dream a dream and to try to analyze it is out of the question, because the Quest has nothing to do with a dreamer! The man who would pursue the Quest of the Self never questions the eternality of the Self, or the perfection of the Self, or the Ideal of the Self. The Self is Omnipresent Knowingness, whether "you" know it or not. The Self can appear as a prompting that causes man to question. The answers given from the standpoint of the Self cause man to see *in*voluntarily, without having to reason, how by being present [i.e., in the company of a Sage], he can be given an intuitive answer that can save him years or centuries of work. The answers, if accurate, are all due to Insight.

People will go to the desert, people will go to the mountaintop, people will go to the caves, people will go to hell and back, trying to find answers to their questions. But unless their questions point directly to man's innate Self-satisfying satisfaction as a Child of the Living Light, they are only causing him to grope through the tunnels of time or through the tunnels of the pyramid with the hopes of salvation sooner or later. All the while the great sepulchre is prepared and waiting to receive another dust body back to its dust origin.[12]

> Joseph: How does "flow" relate to consciousness?

---

[11] Gautama was a manifestation of Buddha, the Divine. Jesus was a manifestation of Christ, the Divine. Buddha and Christ are One.

[12] The implication here is that there is no time to waste for one who's serious about realizing the Self. Also, one needs to be very alert to the type of question asked. Will the answer lead to the pyramid of mentally constructed blocks, or beyond the mind's entanglements?

"Flow" is a suggestion that Consciousness could move or not move from the Point That IS. It is only in the becoming stages that man talks about flow. When man has moved beyond the becoming stages, he sees that his individual "flow" has joined the sea [i.e., C, or Consciousness]. In this marriage, he lives happily ever afterwards.

Joseph: Thank you. What's the right understanding of the Kundalini?

Kundalini refers to the suggestion of a physical embodiment, the belief of a physical arousal, the belief of physical creation, and the suggestion of physical energy. The great power of the Kundalini is termed the Creative Might when fully realized and found to be wearing the garment of Cosmic Consciousness as a constant, with no comment about it!

Joseph: What should I do when it happens?

Ask to whom the Kundalini raises its head. The power may surge through the body of suggestion, but in the celebration of the Feast and in the satisfaction of having gone to the altar of Light, man realizes that the power and the feeling of its arisal points to that moment when you may close the portals of the Soul [i.e., the eyes—outer vision] and see through the opening of the Gate [i.e., the Third Eye—inner vision] that Ra rides again.[13] It is through Self-recognition that you know what it is that truly lives. Very important point.

Joseph: How do I know when sexual feelings are aggressive suggestions and not the power of Love?

The Power of Love is Omnipotent. Sexual arousal often tends to limit Love to matter intercourse. Of course, intercourse may take place, but Love isn't in matter.

Joseph: Thank you. How can two people approach the One in their sexuality?

They can't. Sexuality has arisen as the complaint of the Ages, because of the belief in two. You can't divide One.

---

[13] Ra: the supreme Deity of ancient Egypt, the Sun God. This supreme Spirit in Christendom is known as the Christ or the Word made Flesh.

> Joseph: What is the meaning of mastery of self?

Technique. And when you have accomplished, you will be called an artist, and others will say, "What a work, what a master work that is accomplished." Be One.

> Joseph: Mr. Mills, would you say something about the Evangelical vows of poverty, chastity, and obedience?

Poverty, chastity, and obedience. Obedience means to do the Will, and that is the Law fulfilling chastity and poverty. Poverty is not a suggestion of being without; it has to do with being fully satisfied within. Poverty is the lack of limits, the lack of beliefs. Poverty, in a sense, is like being humble. Know that in the humility commensurate with the Prophet Bird,[14] man may speak the song of a bird, write with the wing of its body, and pen the line in such a way that he activates the golden rule, loves as the gold is seen, and with the attitude of purity finds the great C of chastity. In being Self-seen, man is Self-pure. Where in the Light of Love are the three? They are turned into one. Chastity, poverty, and obedience fulfill the tonal demands commensurate with the string that must vibrate with a Universal Pitch, enabling those who are attuned to it to be found performing in the Symphony of Soul. How do you view chastity, poverty, and obedience?

> Joseph: I look at obedience as listening, poverty as no fuss, and chastity as love.

I would look upon obedience as listening and doing; poverty as no fuss, because there is no fission, only fusion; and chastity as that state of consciousness which can acknowledge Love as All, in spite of verbal declarations about what love is claimed to be about in the land.

> Joseph: What is the correct way to phrase this: "Christ in me" or "me in Christ"?

Neither. Forget about "me" and then find what Christ is. You will only know the Christ in Self-recognition. As long as you have your

---

[14] The "Prophet Bird" has no other purpose but to sing the praises of God-Being and to reveal man's True Nature.

"me" about, you will never find how the captive is set free by being freed from the dreams about the "you" and the "me."

> Joseph: Why can't the psychic realm be found in the land of the Real? And what is the connection between the psychic realm and matter?

The reason the psychic realm can't be found in the land of the Real is that the Real can't be divided. The psychic realm arises from the belief that there is division. The interesting fact about this fiction is that there is really no division. That is why the energy of the psychic field can be translated as the Divine.

> Joseph: Gurdjieff talked about conscious suffering. Is there any conscious suffering?

Yes.

> Joseph: What is the right understanding of conscious suffering?

See if there is a "me" to suffer, if there is a *conscious* "me" to suffer. You see, suffering is merely the belief that there is a "conscious me" who has to go beyond suffering. Conscious suffering is the suggestion that consciousness is personal, human. Consciousness is the only link between this and That; it is neither personal, human, nor Divine. It is the bridge over which man walks into That State of Light, which is called C-o-n-s-c-i-o-u-s.

> Johnny rode a long time ago on his horse so white;
> Johnny rode so long ago, and they call it now on the planes
>        of Light;
> Johnny rode so long ago that men talked about the man,
> So Johnny rides once again, fulfilling the mass demand.
>
> Johnny rides; can you see him? Some see only a horse.[15]
> Can you see a rider, or a rider and no horse?

---

[15] Horse of the mind.

Or can you see a horse, no rider; there is no rider [16] to this policy of That,
Because *this* [17] is the full assurance that Light is the Power; John is the Love, and we post to That.

Joseph: I don't know how to formulate this one. If the power behind dying is One, then how can the human will cooperate? What is the human will?

The human will results from the power claimed befitting living a lie, terminating in death. To terminate means to come to an end, and as soon as possible . . . is all there is to the instantaneous knowingness that Life is All! The suggestion of dying is due to a lapse of consciousness commensurate with a belief termed a believer. So, to die consciously is to cease believing. When you cease believing, find death if you can.

Joseph: Thank you. How can the sixth seal be opened?

By dying to the belief that you think personally about something that has nothing to do with matter: intuition. It will then start to open. It is intuition that brought you here. Your seal is open, but you can't open it for anyone else. It was your seal that got you here, and you might say I sealed it up tight. You will never be able to "leak" again! You will never be able to say you weren't here. You may wish you were not sometimes, but of course you'll just remember St. Francis holding the dove — there he is looking down at you as the little dove, saying, "There's nothing you can do about it, feathered friend; we are from the same Kingdom of Light. I know that Love is All, but I still don't understand how you can appear a bird, and me a man, and yet we do talk . . . one to one."

Joseph: Just one more question. What is the meaning of acknowledgment and worship?

Acknowledgment is the power that enables man to genuflect. Worship is the power of prayer, which would cause him to bend and enable him to find the meaning of "Well done, My good and faithful servant,

---

[16] No personalization; no "person" as a rider.

[17] The Unfoldment.

inherit Now the Kingdom prepared for those who love God, find God, and who know God to be Three as One, appearing as fifty-eight different faces multiplied by infinity to fulfill the Tongue of the Flame."[18]

From Age to Age the Flame has been passed, and man has called it the Torch of Truth, which sets man free from the beliefs of a Miss Liberty—such hollow emptiness![19] Man can only truly find freedom and the totality of Being in the Hall of Knowingness, where God's Gift is acknowledged and man worships at the Altar of Light, knowing the risen Fire has brought the faces to shine so that each may see the facet commensurate with the demand of his inner promptings. When He comes Who can set man free, where will you then find captivity?

There is no division between Heaven and earth, and it is a suggestion that harmony is only a Heavenly experience, seldom experienced on earth. We now know that when two or three are gathered together, or five, six, seven, or eight, there am "I" in the midst.

We are now re-engaging, so it would seem, and stabilizing in this centre of the Work that must be fulfilled in the formality of a setting commensurate with the Form beyond all suggestions of frailty, and lighted by the spontaneous promptings of Joy. We know what Jesus meant when he said, "If ye have seen me, ye have seen the Father." Man calls, and in the plea of the mass finds fulfillment in a living Principle involuntarily experienced, all because All is Love.

In the Power of His Holy Name have we conducted this service and this Eucharistic offering. The Altar of Light overlooks the temple of time, garmenting it until that moment when the temple of time shall be swallowed up in belief and found to be a living Temple. Right there in the midst am "I".

Those who have listened to me in the frequency common to those at my side, may they declare they were present as the wing of the bird dips into the pool and man finds the Tongue of the Flame. In this service, the heart is found no longer bleeding, but acknowledges that blessed State in which man can conceive immaculately the nature of Christ.

---

[18] Reference is made to the Diamond, a symbol of the pure, unadulterated Consciousness. The flame in a diamond is only perceived when there is light. The "Tongue of the Flame" is the Word.

[19] Liberty can never be limited by form.

[Those present in the room give their names.]

You may hear this tape again, Joseph. Listen to it carefully. No human mind is capable of understanding what was said tonight, because no human mind gave it to a human mind to understand. What is understood points to the record that has been written.

Joseph: I shall never forget this night.

Nor I, Joseph. Isn't it strange for people to ask, "Does Mr. Mills acknowledge?" I acknowledge all the time, but I don't acknowledge a "guide" as such, because I know of no Guide but One. Yet, this seems to bother people. There is no "channel" to Truth, to Being, unless of course you wish to become a tributary. I would suggest that you give up all suggestions of being a tributary and be One.

I don't know, Joseph, what you are going to do with these ideas. From the standpoint of Joseph, I have no idea what you will do with the answers to your questions, which you have heard tonight. But I hope you will know how you will live your life as a result, despite your accomplishment in the realm of metaphysics, mysticism, and Sufism. You have come here under the promptings of something happening within you, and it should lead to something powerful.

This is happening and this is all beginning to unfold for you in the "gathering place," which is what "Toronto" means in the language of the Indians. The five senses are represented by the five lakes. The flatlands are golden in the harvest light, and there are many who would eat of the Bread. The Light is ever present. Man must see how there is no underground passage through which he has to crawl to find illumination. He only needs to come out of suggestions, out of the pyramid of doubt, and find how the Stolen Cap[20] is replaced in the power of knowingness as the Great Hood is donned once again.

There is more going on in your consciousness, Joseph, than you have any idea of. This Unfoldment is something that no speculatory science can ever understand, but the day will come when you will find your consciousness completely moved. This is why no one should come unless he has sincerity. You have no idea what you are touching.

---

[20] The Stolen Cap points to the personalization of Wisdom, which thwarts the ultimate accomplishment of liberation.

Also, the movement that you are experiencing in consciousness has to be carefully protected. Once the consciousness begins to open, it should not be tampered with by engaging in psychological, mystical, or drug involvements.

Well, I've never had such questions asked of me. But now you are responsible for the answers!

> Joseph: I have felt all night that my tears, you know, were just like tears of joy. The thing that keeps coming into my mind is "The day is ended, the Day is One."

This is just my life.

## The Picture Presentation

*As long as you are conscious
of the Consciousness
that lights up your experience,
you are conscious of the garment
of the Self.*

## 11     The Picture Presentation

November 8, 1973, New York City

This is the evening of November 8, 1973, at a place found in a city of cement where man cries out by vocalizing through the corridors of time how to arrive at the year of the Lord all together. It is well that we are having this session recorded, because you see that the plants can't talk and the roses can't talk,

> And "you" and "me" will never know what I have said;
>     only the roses can tell
> That they know how to come to bloom, having passed through
>     the stem where the barbs of suggestion dwell.
>
> So, now we see that Wendy W. has come by the trail
>     as planned;
> She came from *New* Canaan[1] and not the old, dreamed up
>     by a "liberated" man.
> And she knew the Cana of Galilee,[2] and she knew and has
>     come to see
> How it happens that one can grow up and become one full
>     of the art To Be.

---

[1] In the Metaphysical Bible Dictionary (written by Charles Fillmore and published by the Unity School of Christianity, Montana, 1931), Canaan is shown to have come from a Hebrew word meaning "realized nothingness; material existence; traffic in materiality; a merchant; a pirate; low; inferior; lowland." (p. 138) The book further defines "Canaan" as the "body consciousness." When the body consciousness is redeemed, that is, seen for what it really is, it becomes the "Promised Land," referred to in the text as "New Canaan." Wendy was living in New Canaan, Vermont at the time of this meeting with Mr. Mills. The "liberated man" refers to Moses. He was "liberated" only to the extent of leading the people into the Promised Land, but he himself was denied entrance.

[2] In the Metaphysical Bible Dictionary (p. 137–8), "Cana" is derived from a Hebrew word meaning "place of reeds; reed; cane; staff; spear; measuring rod; rule; balance; hollow tube." Metaphysically, it is described as "the power centre in consciousness" and has to do with the voice ("reeds" symbolizing the vocal chords).

So, keeping it simple and straightforward, the direct route
    came on the wheel as planned,
And you held the reins of your mighty charger and appeared
    in the house as planned.[3]
So, in the name of the roses and the paradise bird and the candle
    that glows at our side,
We welcome you to this place, where we sit and chat in the
    Light and abide.

So, you will say, "What under the sun is he talking about?"
    and that is always a question of the time;
I'll tell you right now that what I am talking about only points
    to what I am *not* talking about, and that's how "I"
    come about in time.
So, in this rhythm of action you will say, "I don't know
    what's happening at all,"
But we only know this mighty fact, that when you think,
    that is how man falls.
If you think you're a thinker and fall for the suggestion
    of being a thinker in time,
You cannot help but be tied in knots, instead of being
    a known Point simply divine.

"Now what is he talking about, a Divine Point?" this child
    is apt to say.
Well, I will tell you right now, Truth is usually discerned
    or divined in an unusual way.
It sometimes takes a moment to catch up with what you have
    divined,
But I can tell you right now, when you hear the sound, you will
    know, and then will you have divined?[4]

So, this is how it is happening, and this is how you should be educated in the schools. I'm hoping that in the community spirit you will come to be as you should, but I doubt it.

    The community spirit says you must be active in the way
    Of doing all you can to promote the community spirit
        and its way;

---

[3] Referring, on one level, to Wendy's drive from New Canaan to New York City.

[4] Or will you have perceived what and where the Divine is?

But there is only One Spirit, which bears the community
of all the Saints and Sages of man,
And this is the one that I talk about; it's part of a recorded
and yet unseen Plan.

I draw upon the recorded and I bring into soundingness
the Chord,[5]
And it is only suggested fiction that says you are a "repeat"
and on a shore.[6]
What truly has happened is like when you go to sleep
some night, you know,
And you say, "I'm going to sleep, and then tomorrow
I'll awake and get on with the show."
But you know when you awaken in the morning, what put
you to bed at night
Is the same thing that wakes you up in the morning and tells
you everything is all right.

And that's Love.[7] And that's what this is all about, because unless man comes to Love and Love comes to man, man doesn't know what it is to be Love's Man or Man's Love.

It is so nice that a woman like you can enter onto the field of liberty and can appear to choose your courses so that you can find your consciousness aligned to what you like best. In this way you will be able to discriminate and find what may be helpful in fulfilling your life action. Know that all the books that you have studied and all the courses that you have taken point to the possibility of your coming into the awareness of a pattern [i.e., of any new experience] that you say you are coming to know, all because you were attentive. This is the whole point, you see: as long as you *think* about a situation, the situation only remains as thought about. The best way to find a "releasement" from the suggestion of a good situation or a bad situation is to adhere to One Point [i.e., the Absolute, the I AM] and find no relative position or situation.

Now, when you know that two and two is four, you never have to be concerned about anyone who believes it to be five. You stay with a

---

[5] Triad of Being: Life, Truth, Love.

[6] Reincarnated into materiality.

[7] An aspect of the I AM (Life's Omnipotent Verities Eternal).

fixed point. You know that two and two is four, and it doesn't matter whether your mother says it's five, or your father says it's five, or all your friends say it's five. You just say, "Well, if you want to go on thinking that, go right ahead, but I know that two and two is four, and I don't have to stay in after school to prove it!"

Yet, this is what people do with their lives. They swear something is so when it isn't so, and consequently have to go about continually trying to prove something to be that isn't so. As a result they eventually end up underground, instead of flying in the Resurrected Consciousness, which Jesus the Christ promised would be possible for all men who realized that "I and my Father are One." In acknowledging this fact, they could move into the frequency of an experienced situation upon the mountain of observation, where all the suggestions of magnitude[8] are seen as relevant or relative to the standpoint of the one viewing the happening.

Now, if you view a motion picture, perhaps in Radio City Music Hall, you will find that what you see on the screen and what you see on the stage is all relative to the light. And you say, "Oh yes, thank goodness that there is a projection booth behind the third balcony, that there are spotlights that can light up any balcony, and that there is a screen upon which a picture can be projected," which enables you to say, "Well, I spent the evening at the movies and I'm just a wreck, because I empathized with the heroine or the hero to such a degree that now I cannot find any sense of peace. I seem to have suffered right through everything he or she did."

This is the way a lot of my friends used to speak to me, and I have heard those in my family say the same thing. But consider this: if you view something happening on the screen, the only reason you see it is that the light/Light is there. The fascinating part is that in order to see what is happening on the screen, the light in the auditorium has to go down. Only then can the pictures passing before the projected light be discerned.[9]

So, the pictures stop when the film is over and the lights go up in the auditorium. But the people never think to say, "I would never have

---

[8] For example, the suggestion that Truth could be approached and experienced from a personal standpoint, thereby creating the illusion that the person is more glorified.

[9] The pictures on the screen are like the world. In order for the world to be seen and related to as a limited, objective phenomenon, the light of awareness and understanding has to be dim or dimmed. When the "light" is turned on again, the illusions or "pictures" fade.

seen that moving picture if it hadn't been for the stability of the screen upon which those moving pictures could be shown." And that stable screen can be likened unto the Light of your Consciousness. You will *never* be deprived of your conscious Light, and on that screen of conscious Light you see me, Christopher, Jaan, yourself, all your friends, and all your world as it moves before the projection booth of mind. The Light of Consciousness is the Substance of Life as the Self. As long as you are conscious of the Consciousness that lights up your experience, you are conscious of the garment of the Self. When you are aware of what constitutes the Consciousness, then you become aware of what *is* the Self. When you have reached that point of knowing what constitutes the Self and consciously experience the constituents of the Self, you have experienced Self-Consciousness.[10] And this is the great aim of the quest of the man or woman who would enter the Path of the Uncontradictable. It's as simple as that. It's so simple.

When you have experienced this Self-Consciousness, it far transcends the body-self. The body-self is only a figment of the Light. It's a fragment of the Light projection. When you have experienced yourself as Conscious Being and not only as physical embodiment, you must hold onto that Point, and that is what we call the "Narrow Gate." You must hold it open, because all the human opinions and beliefs, all the human thoughts, would try to close it. You see, if you transcend the human and then don't empathize with everyone who has a complaint, they will complain that you are cold and indifferent. Seldom will they support your new stand.

When people come to you and ask you to share their sorrow or share their joy, just know that the only thing you can do is be the Light to what they would call their sorrow or their joy. The Light of Consciousness knows neither state, but enlightens both. It's the awareness of That Which IS that enables you to say, "I AM the Joy and I AM the Happiness, which, if not recognized, appear as the sorrow of mankind."

Sorrow, lack of joy, and lack of happiness are all due to throwing up a screen[11] instead of pulling up the curtain. The Screen (Consciousness) always exists; you only have to raise the curtain and claim the Electrical Force commensurate with the Heart of the Atom of Light.

---

[10] "Constituents of the Self" refers to body, world, and universe. From the standpoint of the Self these are known as they really are. They are seen as not being separate from the Self.

[11] In this instance, "screen" refers to the mind-screen, the seat of misidentification.

And so, Wendy has had a visit, and you might say, "What an invitation!" because in the invitation to come *in*, to be welcomed and seated, man finds himself in the auditorium of the operation called the nine of action.[12] Love is the fulfilling of the Law, and the cement that binds is not the cement of the buildings that constitute a city, but it is the Love that constitutes the Being claimed I AM.

No matter where you go, people may now say, "Wendy, who are you?" And you can reply, "What?! I am Wendy." But you know that you declare who you really are when you declare "I am." You wouldn't say, "I am [AM] sick," but you might say, "Wendy is sick." I AM couldn't be sick, because you couldn't imagine Consciousness as it IS being sick. Consciousness declares itself in the declaration "I am." Consciousness is limited and conditioned when called Wendy, Kenneth, Jaan, or Christopher.

So, if Wendy is sick, let Wendy take an aspirin. It isn't the cure-all or the end-all, but the All is the beginning and the end, and it's not a pill! It is the solution to the problem of Being. It is found in acknowledging the Power of Love, which wipes away all tears from man's eyes. The promise of the Age is that the Power of Love will reactivate the energy fields commensurate with the Man of the Universe and the Glory that surrounds the radiation of the Sun/Son. In this day, man can say he walks in the sunshine of knowing that the Child of Love is conceived in the womb chamber of a thought filled with expectancy and awaiting the Visitation of the Dove.

Thus endeth this formal greeting with Wendy as she wonders what under the sun appears winged on the blue horizon, which is finding its way into her sounding chamber of consciousness, beating upon the strings of her heart. It is interesting that Wendy should come at this time, because her life stands before her.

---

[12] According to Mr. Mills, "nine" signifies Law and Will.

## Moving Furniture Around

*Listen wisely
and worship no person.
Worship
and adore the Self.*

## 12    Moving Furniture Around

February 20, 1975, Berkeley, California

It is going up the chimney, which is where all smoke should go [referring to the smoke from the incense]. The fire should be going. Why don't you put the incense over here so the people can enjoy it. You know, it is one thing that we all have in common, the fragrance of the one stick.

This is February 20, 1975. I see a few new faces, so the story goes. Some have said that those who would engage the path of Self-discovery are either in the category of water-logged logs, dry wood, charcoal, or gunpowder. But you know, to categorize is to limit. It provides an excuse for you to continue to be what you know you are not, while claiming you are hoping to be what you really are. You see, if you find That for which you seek, you will have no excuse to continue being a searcher, and you will not support all those who thrive on searchers. You may appear to be the "open sesame" [i.e., a guiding force, a living answer] for those who would ask you about the light that has come into your eyes and how it started. And you can say, "It was prepared before me, for it is stated in one Book of Power that 'I go to prepare a place for you.'"[1] It is this State that is acknowledged and it is in this framework that the Unfoldment glows in the joy of acknowledging "I and my Father are One" and "Consciousness is fundamental and what you are conscious of constitutes your experience." The healing hands today are laid not on the physical body, but on the mental body, for it is there that you must exchange the thoughts that would bind you for those thoughts commensurate with the Divine Ideal, which you must structure according to your inner promptings. You will find your practice laid out for you when you start to flex the muscles of your thought realm. Find only those thoughts that are acceptable in the Light of the Ideal entertained in the light of attention.

None of this is new to you, I am sure. You have studied many books and you have heard so many people speak about the same topic that it is no wonder that "you" is forever the topic of conversation! It is in this "you" environment [i.e., the everyday mind] that we hope to apply the attitudes commensurate with building a New State so that you and your world may

---

[1] John 14:2.

find that Unity can and does exist in practical, worldly expression. A belief that is no longer held by believers fades in the living Principle Power, which unites all suggested divisions [categories] of those who dream. It is in this attitude that we say we must find the Self. Only then can we hope to find or show another.

These words that I speak are not new at all. They point to a *fire*, and to the apparent lack of the proper conditions needed for an immediate blaze that would consume the sodden legacies of the past. You who are mystically inclined and astrologically inclined are expecting to see the Urn Bearer of the Aquarian Age walk across the sky, overturning the contents of his urns, which consists of the watery nature [i.e., the feminine aspect of consciousness], the stars [high aspirations], the moon [feminine pole], and the sun [masculine pole]. All of these phases of consciousness must once again be brought back into perspective with their Origin or Source.[2] This sounds so terribly serious, because you look so serious. If you look at me and are casting mental judgments upon my physiognomy, remember that I am like a reflector that reflects what you look like from my point of view! So, the log crackles as it dies — I hope you will!

You know, when you ask someone to help you move your furniture around, *you* have to live with it. In the rearrangement of the furniture, you say your room feels like new. It seems very nice for a moment, but then if you decide that you don't like living with the new seating arrangement, you call upon another friend to help you drag your furniture back to its more familiar place. Then you do not have to consider relocating your position of love [love-seat], your wings [wing chairs], or your table in a room unfamiliar to you.[3]

It's very interesting, you see, everyone talks, and those who are searching for a new arrangement are usually asking to hear a variation on the themes "I and my Father are One" and "I AM That I AM." If these themes are enunciated in your arrangement, which you have ordered for the day in which you seem to live and move and have your being [i.e., your incarnation], you must strive to keep those themes of melodic significance ever discernible, regardless of the embellishing tones that surround your

---

[2] Both the universe within and without must be seen in relation to (i.e., not separate from) the Self.

[3] This illustration is most meaningful when the "furniture" is considered as *mental* furniture, that is to say, concepts, beliefs, ideas, thoughts, emotions, etc., which fills one's room of consciousness.

course through the unfolding pattern called life.[4]

There are some who compose variations in which you can seldom recognize the hidden theme of significance. When you ask where it is hidden, you may be given the reply, "It is there if you can catch the harmonic structure and follow the internal design." Beethoven wrote thirty-two C minor variations, but unless you have another piano and a performer always playing the original theme, in some of those variations it is very difficult to find the theme, for it seems to escape the scheme. It is the same with a set of variations I know by Copland.

Now, those who are bringing into expression ways and means of arriving at the Source must forever be in the position commensurate with birth, for receptivity and humility must be apparent. You can say, "I will think anything I wish," and it is so. But if you are practising your abstract exercises in order to develop a technique so that you can "die" when it comes to actual performance, you will have the awareness to say, "I know I think, but not so. I must *know* that my tones [thoughts] are commensurate with the Key [Principle] that I have assigned to hold a position in my experience, which is unfolding for those who see me as a product of horizontalization."[5]

As you know, the log on the fireplace was once upright and bore leaves and branches as the result of roots. When it had fulfilled its purpose, you laid the axe to its comfortable position and felled it. It is now found upon your hearth with the hopes that you might find a means of bringing it together with a chemical reaction [i.e., the match] and thus find a transcendent experience in the wood bursting forth in flame and revealing the energy inherent beneath its bark.

So, you hear all the "barkers" [i.e., talkative innovators of the day], and you hear this one. But I tell you now, the only reason I utilize the vocal chords is to hear my Self speak. And I share this with you, for you have

---

[4] Truth must be discerned and held to in the midst of worldly affairs. The demand is for Truth to be clearly understood. Only then can it remain "ever discernible."

[5] Horizontalization involves process, hence a progression. It has to do with the mind's sequential interpretation of Reality (based on notions of time and space, cause and effect). Indeed, everyone's experience could be said to "unfold." However, Reality as it IS, the I AM, if compared with the concept of horizontalization, has to be considered to be *vertical,* that is, beyond sequence, process, notions of time and space, cause and effect, etc. There is no process to the I AM, no sequence. It is already complete, perfect in its state of eternal Nowness.

asked to hear me speak. I am perfectly satisfied just to be quiet, or to raise the roof, all according to the note of melodic significance [or the demands of horizontalization]. One note strategically placed can lift the lid of your mental crypt. We saw this last evening, and unfortunately the one who experienced it isn't here. Perhaps she decided to draw back into the sarcophagus, but let us hope that she hasn't, for last night was a moment when she moved into a pattern of awareness knowingly, and everyone in the room rejoiced in the warmth of the fire. It was well laid.

    I did not know this one, so time would say, but One (the "I," of course) does not know divisibility, but in Its All-encompassing or Omnipotent Power, It embraces what appears as everything, including you. The difficulty happens when you try to use your equipment to fell the tree of accomplishment without fulfilling the law of obedience. Someone once said that fulfilling obedience is the first law of accomplishment. Another simple but important statement: "To thine own Self be true and then how can thou be false to any man?" In that state, where is the false man to be found? And if found, the false face is discerned, and you know the fun of unmasking when the clock strikes twelve. You have lived long enough holding up your disguise. You may now say within yourself, "The time has come to pass, and my face falls. What is there written as the lines?"[6]

    It is a very musical evening. I hope you are musically oriented. If not, start taking piano lessons under a well-disciplined teacher! You may be naturally gifted in playing the piano, but the gift of technique enables you to become superfluous by being one with the instrument so that what is contained within its box may fill the room and point the way to the Theme of soundingness, which has been stated to soar "on the wings of song" and has been recorded as the Master's Voice. The dog knew enough to listen. Do you? [laughter]

    Now, I must tell you that most people don't like me to laugh at my own jokes. It bugs them. But after all, you need some abrasive surface on which to scratch and get rid of your chemical head! You may find upon striking it within yourself that your heart turns over as your *head* begins to feel. When this happens, your heart begins to beat another rhythm entirely, and you can say, "I march in rhythm with the tide of events commensurate with the Promise that all men should be free when found alive in the Light of the Eternal." Of course, that has nothing to do with your face, the lines.

---

[6] The face is referred to here as the canvas of experience; the lines are the brush strokes. A music staff also comes to mind—what is the melody written when the disguise falls?

And so your clef [from the Latin word *clavis:* key] must have a staff,[7] and may you find the Grand Staff, which enables you to appear like music in an Age when each one thinks his own chromatic situations bear significance.[8] Of course, they have only appeared to be resolved due to the Law of Action [i.e., Karma]. You might say, Karma appears, musically speaking, to be like a chromatic situation in which one thinks in terms of rows all bearing crosses, instead of in terms of the Rose.[9]

You know, it is stated that men and women should be given the keys to the Kingdom of Light. But how under the sun can you expect to have the keys when "you" persist and drag your skeleton along [i.e., body identification, the crosses]! The key to all doors [i.e., the skeleton key] appears like a work of wonder, but in order to work, it must have the ability to unlock the inner recesses of thought. The thought must be found to be the means by which "I" am recognized. Then "you" die in the joy of being found a flame in the name of that Light [i.e., Jesus] who said that all men should be filled with joy and that their cups should be running over, for surely goodness and mercy shall follow those who would be receptive and bear the patience and humility to practise. The demands of an inspired Source asking to be cognized must be engaged in the experiencing of your questioning natures.

As they say, "a stairway to the stars"—it doesn't have to be a spiral one [i.e., a circuitous one]. Don't believe; if you do, you are in the process of structuring such a staircase. Instead, acknowledge what you know to be true and live what you have found to be true, even if it is only "two plus two." It's the beginning of knowingness. Numbers can't free you, but they do reveal how you and your teachers can die to having opinions.[10] Fan the

---

[7] The clef or key is like Principle, which must have a "staff" or field of expression (world activity) to appear practical.

[8] Grand Staff: Higher, God-oriented field of activity in life. One who has found the Grand Staff can move beyond the chromatic situations of time (i.e., limited, personal field of action).

[9] The "rows," aside from their obvious reference to the graveyard, can also be seen as the twelve-tone rows that one finds in modern music, which are melodies that have no key centre (no recognition of I AM). The "crosses" signify conflicting paths followed by different persons, each person "doing his own thing." The cross also denotes identification with the physical body. "The Rose" symbolizes Realization. It is like the opened, liberated Consciousness when freed from erroneous identifications.

[10] "Two plus two" illustrates, in a simple way, how Truth is beyond deliberation or opinions.

embers of the Indivisible or Individual Life. It lies waiting to receive the Light of the Age in which you think you live and move. Listen, for you will hear what the Stars [i.e., Masters of Ages past] have said when they came tumbling down upon your stage in time. They will not be shouting, "Barabbas!"[11] They are always shouting, "A new Star is born." "No man knoweth when 'I' cometh." I say unto you: "Watch!"

Well, this is the way I talk to the new people. It doesn't usually sound so "heavy," but at least you now have some idea of what I seem to be like. As you gain some idea of what I am not like, your only hope is to come to terms with your own "furniture arrangement"! Let me simply enjoy the Theme upon which I embellish involuntarily, for it has been fun to sit in your parlor, appearing to lounge amid what I claim to be the infinite resources of spontaneity. You might call what you have heard so far the exposition or the enunciation—it all depends whether you've heard it as a fugue or a sonata.

You know, I gave a deceptive cadence in the middle of this talk when I mentioned how people can't stand it when I start to laugh, especially at my own jokes. That cadence is still unfinished. In other words, I am telling you that it must be resolved, for it was sounded. Everything you think in silence is as noisy as the very devil [i.e., like the "chromatic situations"]. You know, many people have touched the cards of chance with the hopes of interpreting them without knowing anything about their origin. Did you know that the Aquarian pack of Tarot Cards apparently has the devil as the "thinker"? So, have a great time!

A few of you appear a little sleepy this evening. If you are tired, you must know it doesn't have a thing to do with your liberation. It only points to where "you" are. If you are enjoying yourself in spite of your fatigue, there's hope! You know, you can never go by feeling tired, because tiredness is always a suggestion that would keep you from Being. One great metaphysician I knew once said, "Fatigue is the worst enemy of the metaphysician." This is true, yet most metaphysicians appear to be "metafizzles." They tend to get inundated with intellectual, abstract exercises with the hopes of being semi-free instead of "home safe."

[To the stenographer]: Am I going slow enough tonight, Rose? Sometimes the words are like bullets. Of course, some of you know that; you

---

[11] The students of the Pacific School of Religion (on whose campus Mr. Mills gave this Unfoldment) were currently preparing a play entitled "Barabbas" as part of their Easter festivities.

got "shot" on Sunday![12] But others have just sort of come in on a wing and a prayer with one engine missing—as one light is [Mr. Mills points to the chandelier in the room]. I must give you some electric light bulbs. Apparently you don't have enough in the storeroom.

> Elizabeth T.: Thank you, in advance.

Oh, you'll get them, dear!

> Dr. Wilhelm (Bill) W.: We need the money to pay for the bill. We can afford the light bulb, but not the bill that comes.

You *can* afford the light bill. There is always a price to the Light, and that's just the point. How many are willing to pay the price for the Light? As long as one thinks he is a Bill/bill, instead of the Will I AM, there exists the question! Remember, when I use the word "I", I am not referring to me. If I were, I would be relieving you of a tremendous amount of responsibility!

> Elizabeth T.: You mentioned two words that are big for me, "receptivity" and "humility." We often hear people saying that some people are not too receptive.

Water-logged.

> Elizabeth T.: Some are proud and not humble. If such a person is in quest for such beautiful qualities as receptivity and humility, how will that person go about it?

If he has receptivity and humility, "proudness" is undoubtedly the wrong word. The right word might be "confidence." Usually, when you are humble and ready to receive, you are not wishy-washy or like a marshmallow. You are confident. Confidence is being quiet, but assured. But if one is proud and is lacking in humility and receptivity and yet is engaged in the Quest, you might say it is only in the name of the Quest that he is searching. Such a one only wishes to be in vogue and has no hopes of being reborn consciously into a pattern commensurate with the Ideal, or anything like that. Many say they are on the Quest, because it is the thing to do today. It's the

---

[12] Referring to the Unfoldment Mr. Mills gave on that particular day.

"in" thing. Really, it is the "out" thing.

Hope is always whispering, if you really are seeking. Find your Self and don't speculate about the proud ones. There will always be a film made in their glory.[13] There will be no film made when you find your Self, because there will be no need of a projection booth to furnish proof that you have a figure needing to be photographed in order to convince people you are around.

Tom D.: Mr. Mills, can I ask a question?

Yes.

Tom D.: Who are you?

That is the question that all seekers ask when they are trying to identify themselves through the agency of an external speaker. It is better to ask *"What* am I?" and die to the figuration that you give unto a note that has claimed your attention. Look within yourself and ask "What am I?" and then you will know who I am.

Tom D.: Thank you.

You are most welcome.

You know the little old saying when you are trying to grow up
And you have to go to school and it seems to erupt,
And all those little kids that play on your street
Don't always like the rhythm you beat.

So, you have to go to school by yourself.
Sometimes you aren't very large, but others tell
That they are mighty big, and so they bully you around.
And you say: "What am I going to do if I can't run by leaps
    and bounds?"

Then, when you get tired of running the race of life,
You say: "I'm mighty weary, and my feet are sore in strife."
It is common not only to walk barefoot in the park,
But also to run upon the concrete, never finding where "I"
    did start.

---

[13] Referring to a film entitled "The Proud Ones."

And so, you all know the story about the tones of kids,
They always have some rhyme to tell, all because "you" is
Not what they think you are. They have really got to find
What it is that is irking them within their shallow minds!

You can say: "Sticks and stones can break my bones, but
    words will never hurt me."
That's because you are shallow. I tell you now, they hurt thee.

    Watch! and listen to what is spoken unto you by me or by anyone else, and if it cannot be applied to Principle, do not accept it. If it can be applied to Principle, it is impossible to reject. Don't be followers after people. That is the epidemic prevalent among all the kids rushing around trying to get schooled. Listen wisely and worship no person. Worship and adore the Self. In the meantime, the go-between time, bridge the passage with the knowing that "I" love you.

    Remember, you who are under the roofs of this complex situation of campus are hoping that a great unifying action can take place among the great named denominations of your breeding. Know that in the fulfillment of such a dream [i.e., ecumenism], principles are at the root of the accomplishment. Consider well that a principle, to be a principle, must be fixed and immutable. If yours changes, get a move on and run, because you are dealing with the principles of dreamers. If you find the true Principle, then bear the torch, the flame, so that those dead sticks that you may meet can say, "I see a light in your eyes and I wonder why. There is also an all-encompassing aroma...." You can reply, "Oh, yes, I know, for I know that one stick lighted [i.e., a Teacher] gave me the essence of its Body [i.e., Fragrance—Truth] as the energy to my walk through the valley of life."

    You mustn't rest in the valley. Inwardly you must know this, either you wouldn't be perched on the side of this hill! As you know, this basin [i.e., the San Francisco Bay area] catches much from the tide of events. It is well that it be shored, for there is enough loose mental driftwood on the waters of consciousness. May you hear within yourself the ringing of the Bell that forever charts the course as you sail your Ship of Soul (the feeling of Being I AM) through the riptides of suggestion and find the spiralling eddy appearing in the form of a match [i.e., ignition through irritation], and your torch aglow.

    It is serious, as is all music that is considered to be of a classical nature. But of course, there is always the fun music for those who want a scintillating display in order to see what technique has been accomplished. Mine is often serious, however, for I knew the joy of Being alone [i.e., all-One] before I found how "I" love you [i.e., before I found the all-inclusive nature of the "I"].

Consider it well. It's not easy to move this furniture back when it has once been moved, because "you" were not present when I did the moving [i.e., the "you" orientation was silenced in the experience of newness]. So, don't come again unless you are serious, and unless you have no reservations about finding a new position of comfort, substance, and wealth. The price is right, for this new position is blessed and fulfilled in the involuntary action of the Current of Event, loosely called "Light." Good night.

All: Good night, Mr. Mills. Thank you.

It's my pleasure. If I had not spoken to you, I would not have heard it this way. Similarly, if the music had not been written, you would never have heard it played, unless you and the Source were joining hands and applauding the same miracle and wonder of spontaneous action.
All set? What a view you have of your city. I hope you can go into it and out of it at will!

## "My Blasted Intellect!"

*What is laziness?
The intellectual malady that arises
when the intellect
is not engaged
in a directed act.*

# 13     "My Blasted Intellect!"

### April 2, 1975, Tucson, Arizona

This is the evening of April 2, 1975, in Tucson, Arizona, in company with Steve, Jaan, Jerry, and Chris. We are considering a missile, a base, and a centre on the top of the mountain, which may one day appear in the foothills for those who can approach with sincerity the Apex of Light.[1] What are you dying to ask, Steve?

    Steve D.: After that, I'm dying to ask whether you've read a particular book, but I think I'll postpone that one.

What's that? You're dying to ask what?

    Steve: Whether you had read a certain book, but I think it's irrelevant, and I'd best postpone it if not...

It's not irrelevant. Ask me.

    Steve: Well, it has to do with missiles and the images you were just expanding. I'm referring to *Gravity's Rainbow* by Thomas Pynchon. The title of the book refers to the arc of the ballistic missile.

The descent.

    Steve: Yes, but what I was dying to ask was why are so many of us not awake? What was the fall of man? How did we come to be asleep, and why is it so difficult for us to know who we really are?

---

[1] In January, 1976, Kenneth Mills established a centre for his Work in the Southwest. It is called "Arinaka" and is located in the foothills of the Santa Catalina Mountains near Tucson, Arizona.

Well, I could be very sharp, you might say, and strike a blow to the diamond and show you, when it's cut, how the fire is revealed. But they tell us that a perfect diamond has fifty-eight faces and a plateau on top to evidence the power of the reflected light. The idea of men and women being asleep arises from the alibi of behaving as men and women, because somebody asleep told them they were "men and women." And it has passed from generation unto generation, so they say, and that passing has been the passing on of dream data. The awakening facts, however, point to the situation of Man bearing no resemblance to men and women, but to a state of Consciousness uncontaminated and unfettered by the empirical data of time. Your question has nothing whatsoever to do with the true state of Man, because the true state of Man is not a question; it's the answer. It could all be said in two or three words: Your question is relevant as long as you identify with your corporeality and with your thought-mind. Find the Source of the thought that there is a mind called yours, and then see if you aren't awake. It's very simply put.

> Steve: Well, maybe after a warning like that I shouldn't pursue it, but where do these dream data come from? How did they arise in the first place and how did we get trapped in this mode of perpetuating the dream rather than knowing that we can be awake?

Well, you see, when you ask someone in the dream, as you are flying from Tucson to Shangri-la, about the state of things in a place en route, your dream partner will give you the data, and you will take it. You may reach your destination of Shangri-la or you may not, but the interesting thing is, as soon as the alarm goes off, you wake up and begin another day. What you have experienced as a conversation with an unknown dream-friend about the state of affairs in a place on your way to Shangri-la no longer exists, because in the awakened state you no longer know where you were when you spoke to your dream-friend. The place, the dream-friend, and your state are all erased upon awakening. And that is exactly what happens in the experience of what is called realizing the Self, or coming face to face with the Self. You can never account for the dream while being in it, but you can see the transience of it, because it changes constantly. The only thing that doesn't change is the Light to it. Find the Source of the Light, and then see if you will dream on or leave your dreams for joyful awakening. You see, no matter how many questions you ask about the dream, the dream can never be a state that is real, for the Light behind it is the only thing that is real, and you have to find the Source of That.

> Steve: But it's within the dream that one is caught while one is looking for that Light.

It *seems* to be that way, but if it were that way, you would never find it. If you are searching for the Light, you do so by accepting only those thoughts, those states, and those facts into your scheme of reasoning that can be associated with Principle. This Unfoldment is based on the Principle "I and my Father are One *here-now* and not *shall be*; Consciousness is fundamental and what you are conscious of will constitute your experience; I of myself can do nothing; Perfection underlies reality." The Perfect Principle Ideal One is a realization that you are able to hold. It satisfies the errant mind. You train the mind, so to speak, by feeding it those thoughts, or holding it to those thoughts that approximate the Ideal so that when you come face to face with the Ideal as a living, conscious realization, your mind just dies in the embrace of the One Altogether Lovely.

It's so strange that you would be asking me about dreams. It reminds me of the Bolinas weekend, when I was confronted by the dream analyst. She was just incensed and as *she* started to wake up, she became so concerned! She tried to fit the whole weekend into the framework of her dream analysis, and it just wouldn't fit. She started to see that she wasn't moving correctly and was consequently quite challenged. You see, the mind is given such wonderful food to perpetuate its own dream state when the dream is given such a sense of reality. It also temporarily but falsely satisfies the innate self-transcendent faculties that are continually demanding expression and fulfillment. This type of analysis seems to satisfy these faculties because they are utilized, to an extent, as one tries to find a way out of the mind and its states. It is this very search in which one tries to find a means out of the limited mentality that evidences the self-transcendent factor in everyone. But the transcendence will never be fully realized that way, because the mind is so capable of conjuring up anything that you wish. The only way you'll find your way out is to find whether or not what the mind conjures up fades out; if it does, then it can't be real. And when you find That which is Real, you can see how all the conjuring and dreaming can appear to come and go, but you remain fixed. And that's the fun of it. It doesn't annihilate anything, it just releases you from all restrictions surrounding your experience in what appears to be the three-dimensional world, and allows you to be as free as a bird on the wing in *song*, not in the feathers![2]

---

[2] In materiality, limitation.

> Steve: What are the other disciplines, such as various types of meditation—Zen meditation, transcendental meditation—that you find are valuable?

All spiritual disciplines have their place, but the biggest challenge of all is to free yourself from believing that they of themselves can do anything. The best way to meditate is to be consciously aware of tying your shoe or to be consciously aware of cleaning your teeth—of doing everything you do—of taking someone's hand, of putting your arms around someone. That is meditating. But if you are thinking whether or not you want to take someone's hand or embrace someone, why, you are leaving so much in the way of a "tracing" (your mind and its workings) that your action doesn't have power.

> Steve: Yes, well, I understand all this with my intellect, but that's a very long way from being able to practise it. How does one . . .

Practise it? Well now, let me show you. Tell me something, how do you know that it is your intellect that is telling you this? Perhaps your statement is being conjured by the intellect in such a way that it skillfully repudiates your practice of being free as you really are. You see, your intellect is a marvelous tool, but it is often used to fabricate all sorts of excuses, which minimizes your life action. You know very well that if you could be just as you really would like to be, why, you would find your whole experience so different that I would wonder how acceptable you would be in the eyes of those called your friends or acquaintances. You see, you will be part of a very different race or breed of the human as soon as you start operating from a Base that is uncontaminated and situated upon the mountain. You might say that those in the foothills are only aware of what it is to approach That State of Awareness (the Mountain). But when you are in That State of Awareness, you can look right over the foothills. So, you let others approach you, and you can talk to them about the heights, and you can talk to them about where they are at, but never do you consider that you are where you appear to be when you know what you really are. Others will try to confine you, but you must stay where you are, especially in practice. That's meditation. You see, when you meditate—as I tell all my students when we have dokusans[3]—the thoughts keep coming, but the point of counting the breaths, for example, is to be able to watch the

---

[3] A Zen term for private meditation counselling with the Teacher.

thoughts come and then to be able to let them go, but you must hold your count, because only then will it become obvious that *what is happening* has nothing to do with thought or the count. It can't be defined, but it's there enabling you to appear to cognize the thought and the count! And yet it isn't the thought or the count!

Your intellect is a marvelous tool. It might be like what they call an uncut diamond, but it really has been well chiseled by time, and now it's ready to be put into action as you cease to let it limit you. The intellect is a tinker, and yet, what would we do without it?

Steve: What are the many ways in which it can limit one?

By having you question why you're not awake! That's the kind of question I like. But of course it's really blasting out the sand from under your feet. You're going to be standing on solid rock, which waits in its opaque and natural state to pass through the action of becoming a Transparent Stone. The greatest gift that any man can give to men and women is the gift of enabling them to see through the world picture and to see its transparent nature. And that is so much fun.

Steve: You seem to have a great deal of fun.

Oh, I do, I love it! We all do. And this is going to be your privilege also. Your voice is right, your voiceprint is right. You may not think your head is, but whose head is? In this Age, you know, the hearing is beyond the ear, the seeing is beyond the deep limpid pools, and the Soul is the act commensurate with feeling the Being I AM. When I use "I AM," as you know, it isn't meant personally at all; it refers to the "I AM That I AM." And to leave "I AM That I AM" merely as a holy thought is to put off being "I AM That I AM." So, all you say in your simplicity is, as I just said, "I AM That I AM." And they die in disbelief. Ha-ha! Instant death!

You see, the intellect can't cope with it at all, but the fascinating part is that this Work is done between the words. And you know it's happening because of what takes place as a result of hearing these words, which bears little relationship to what you thought was going to happen when you heard the words. This is a very important point. This is why, you see, I'm so very careful to whom I speak, because it takes a mighty strong man to suddenly realize that he is Realized and that he just hasn't accepted the Realization. This awareness immediately puts him in the responsible position of being true to the Self when confronted by the beliefs of the not-Self. And this is why it is wonderful to find the Missile of the Divine uncontaminated by the heads of those states (five senses) which would seduce men and women into believing they were what they are not, and in so believing, finding themselves bearing degrees of accomplishment and supposedly ready for a professional action that really does little to profess what it really means to be schooled. I'm never impressed by degrees.

> Steve: My blasted intellect—wow! I'm stunned. That blew me away—the intellect keeps thinking that it can cope with this knowledge purely in its own terms. By so doing, it precludes me from facing the true implications of the higher knowledge, which would, after all, destroy the intellect.

Destroy the *limits* of the intellect. I don't want "you" to be destroyed so suddenly!

> Steve: And it seems to me that so far the deception has been successful. The intellect is so strong that it can assimilate all this and say, "Fine, we will perceive this just in these logical terms and won't let it affect us."

Well, you see the Light that enables you to make all these statements is untouched by your intellect, and that is the state to remain in while still appearing to be very intellectual.

> Let your intellect do the walking through the pages of the times,
> And let your Self be acknowledged as the Light to what is read on the Scroll beyond the mind.[4]

This is how we behave and operate, we look very normal and natural, but we're far from it! You can't compare the State that IS with anything else. The best way to arrive at it is by seeing what it isn't, and what's left over is That Which IS, and "you" have just appeared to be a catalyst in the hourglass of time as the sands run out and the desert grows cold in the awareness of the Eternal Light, symbolically referred to as the "Sun."[5]

---

[4] Unfoldment of intuition and its teaching.

Oh, you're in a marvelous position—completely vulnerable and yet alive! The beautiful thing is, if you have a beautiful intellect as you appear to have, find how you think it and call it an intellect and you will find yourself truly stunned! And what happens when you're stunned? You see stars. And you'll say, "My Lord, a new star is born and it appears as me!" Oh, you'll have so much to do you won't be able to sit around on your derrière meditating!

Oh, it has been marvelous this past year or so, as we've been getting rid of the callouses on people's soles/Souls!

Steve: What is laziness?

The intellectual malady that arises when the intellect is not engaged in a directed act.

Steve: How can one evidence usefully directed action while one is still trapped in the dream?

That question, of course, arises from the standpoint of a dreamer, and you are no longer in that state so I know you are asking it on behalf of your friends! When your friends appear to you, just tell them that they appear to be in the dream and sustain the dream because they have never felt the point on their butts. *Butt* has to do with an age that has passed,[6] and it usually rides as one of those horns of dilemma: *but* and *if*, you know? "I will do it *if* I can. Oh, I will go with you, *but* I must be devoted to what I think I'm doing." So, your friends, you know, just jog them and show them that *but* and *if* are only used now to sit on and get a jolt! You poor man, those close to you will be stunned because you may no longer be so happy!

Steve: I don't believe you.

Oh no, you'll be marvelous.

---

[5] "Sands running out" and the "desert growing cold" refer to material belief and arid states of mind respectively, which no longer have an appeal to one who has awakened.

[6] Reference is made to the Ram, which according to Mr. Mills is a symbol of obstinacy—an attitude which should no longer be in vogue in this Age.

Steve: Unfortunately, I also don't believe you when you tell me I'm no longer dreaming.

Well, you see it is obvious you aren't, because if you were dreaming, you would never be able to distinguish the dream and the not-dream. And you have just distinguished the dream by recognizing the not-dream.

Steve: When and how did I do that?

By your statement. You sentenced yourself by thinking a thought and found yourself tied in a knot. Isn't it simple? You see, your Divinity, your power, your awareness, is so subtle that the intellect may deny it, but it can't deny the fact that its own existence is due to the Light of Consciousness, which even enables you to have your computed data under the label or head of "Department Intellect." Or you might call it "HAL." You saw 2001.[7] That's HAL, and HAL the computer was, you might say, the counterfeit or falsetto voice trying to gain attention in the realm of David's awareness. And, you see, David doubted HAL's infallibility and Frank, the co-pilot, did not. Consequently, Frank was lost in space, but David was willing to de-computerize himself, which appeared in the movie as his removal of HAL's memory banks. He treated it all very objectively. He just pulled one bank out after another. "I'm losing my mind, David; I'm losing my mind." And David, of course, was shaking and was minus any gravity (personal reference) in the situation and he had to hang on for dear life. So, David succeeded in fulfilling his trip and engaged the fulfillment of his launch into his thought-projection toward the destination Jupiter and to points beyond. And Jupiter, of course, symbolically, is the brotherhood planet. And David is the great Biblical symbol of Love. Frank represents the intellect or the doubting Thomas.

But it doesn't matter how long your Monolith, or in other words, the Unknown, has been buried on the moon part of your consciousness (subconscious) forty feet under the dust. It was solid, like a rock, and you undoubtedly remember that when they landed on the moon they went to the crater and saw this great, huge excavation. And there was the ladder descending into the pit where this stone appeared to be just standing. Then, for those who had eyes to see, that part of the moon was going to be struck by the rays of the sun for the first time in centuries. The music

---

[7] *2001: A Space Odyssey.* A film by Stanley Kubrick. Written by Stanley Kubrick and Arthur C. Clarke.

was very tense, and finally the rays of the sun dawned and gradually moved over the peak on the moon and struck the Monolith. And it gave forth a pitch and everyone grabbed their ears; they couldn't stand it. The unknown, which had remained hitherto undetected, became a living frequency of Sound of universal significance. It bridged a gap (unconsciousness) from the moment the ape closed his lids when he was supposed to be keeping vigil on his members by night. Do you remember? The ape closed his eyes and slept, just like Adam, and my word, there was the Monolith standing. And they all started worshipping it, because in the moment of forgetfulness, they could not account for this something which happened. And what was it? This Monolith was an object not understood in consciousness but solidified in a dimensional, restrictive way, waiting to be freed and given back to the Source from whence it came. The moment that the ape slept was the moment when the Monolith first appeared, because that moment was unaccounted for in knowingness and appeared as an obstruction in sight. It's fascinating when you see it this way. What a picture!

> Chris D.: So in that sense the Monolith represents a block.

It seems a block until it's struck by the Sun, and then it carries the pitch of what? of universal significance or the pitch of the universe. You see, the root meaning of "universe" is "to turn into one." And that's the whole message of the Ultimate: to turn into One. There's nothing but One. And so it is that if men and women look over their horizons of time in this Age of Aquarius, they will be coming closer and closer to the conscious recognition of the Great Truth surrounding an Absolute Premise, which has always been termed by the intellectuals as being absolutely abstract and impractical. But they are now seeing over the horizons of their intellects and are seeing that it is the only solution to their fragmented or sand-like existence, which can be blown by the winds. They are coming to see that the truly practical is what appears as the abstract in act. The truly practical always appears as the abstract in act.[8] So, your act is always practical, and others would say, "How come?" and you'd say, "It's just because I abstracted 'me' from the act of being One Altogether Lovely by the grace of the dawning, the Light of the Sun."

> Jaan K.: My word! It's interesting that the an-

---

[8] "Abstract in act" refers to action that has transcended personal entanglements and duality.

swer you gave to one of Steve's questions about "What are the many ways that the intellect can limit one?" was "By having you question why you are not awake." That is the Monolith.

That is the Monolith with no pitch. It is the dawning of the Light of Truth that reveals the pitch. And the pitch is what? the living frequency of Sound of universal significance, or in other words, the realization of the all-encompassing nature of the "I", which cannot be divided. It is set. We pitch to the "I" and tune our strings accordingly. You see, the Monolith is the Unknown, and you abstracted (extracted) the "me" (personality) from it via awe. All the spacemen were filled with awe when they saw the Monolith in the crater on the moon. When "me" is out of the way, awe is present. But as long as me is in the way, the unexplainable remains a dead, catatonic mystery, symbolized in the movie as the Monolith. So, when the "me" was gotten out of the way via awe, it appeared symbolically as the sun striking the Monolith and giving it life as pitch. Thus, the mystery was explained and the import of the Monolith was consciously realized. It's such a lot of foolishness to think that consciousness could come out of the subconscious. It is such a lot of foolishness to think that order could come out of chaos. Ridiculous. It's not that way at all.

Steve: Do you mean to say that consciousness is—

Is.

Steve: —first?

No! And you call it first. Of course it is. Perfectly right.

Jaan: Oh dear, this is incredible! "Consciousness is first." I just wrote, "The tail doesn't wag the dog. The thoughts do not condition awareness. The dog is first; the tail after. Awareness is first, present now; thoughts always happen after awareness and after experience."

Right. Did you just write that while you were waiting, Jaan?

> Jaan: Yes, just about three or four minutes ago.

He's just read it!

> Jaan: That's what Steve is saying, "Consciousness is first!"

[Tape change]

The evening of April 2, 1975, continuing, and the universe stopped, it seemed, for a moment, but that's how the abstract is practical, because it seemed to stop, but there was no change. What we could do, you see, is put these cassettes on a seven-inch reel, and when you hear the seven-inch reel there will be no break. It's only the intellect that sees it stopping and starting, and that's why when you hear it again on a seven-inch reel, there will be no stopping or starting; it just will go right on. The break is only a seeming happening. If you believe in the break, it's the gap over which you must leap. And this is what you must do, Steve, leap. Your intellect and its great ability is not to be dropped, nor must you even try to drop it. It's impossible. All you have to do is see it for what it is and BE.

> Steve: The intellect seems to be a great weight to carry when making that leap over the gap. It's so heavy, it's so strong, and it will not leap of itself, it will not fly, it is heavier than air and it would do everything possible to keep one from making the leap.

Well, the best way to prepare for the leap is to watch the discursive thoughts when they come to you, and say, "Don't stop coming to me. I'm going to meditate. Don't stop coming to me; I want to know from whence you have come!" Watch those thoughts and see where they are leading you. It works. It does, because you are then able to get rid of any excess thought baggage. The intellect was never meant to be a weight, it was meant to be a springboard—resilient and capable of being utilized in leaping from this to That. And for it to be resilient you must be able to drop any thoughts that do not lead to Realization. These thoughts constitute the weight. So, jump on the springboard and dive! You know, as the Maharishi Mahesh says, "Dive deep! Dive deep within!" He is such a fine man, but I have always wanted to ask him, if I ever see or talk with him again, what he means when he tells you to "dive deep within yourself." What is within you that is deep?

>Jaan: Yes. Diving deep may appear as sweeping the floor or polishing glass or something.

Or making coffee or holding the microphone. That is diving deep, because you always see, if you're on the level that IS, what is really happening. In other words, on the level where IS is the happening, IS is happening! This is the incredible part, being able to watch the happening and appearing to be in it and not in it. That's why it's so much fun.

What are you going to do, Steve, after you have written the composition and your cadence that is perfect? What do you plan to do after this year? Are you graduating?

>Steve: No. I've got another year to go.

Do you? Great! You might be here next year when I come back.

>Steve: Yes. I've been hoping to find an easy and not too time-consuming way of making money so that I can be free to pursue music and anything else that takes my fancy, however I want to pursue it. But I'm so lazy, and my pursuits seem to be so unfocussed that I really wonder sometimes just what I am doing.

You are dreaming up excuses. Polish your wings with Twinkle Bright and fly! Steve, I think, has had experiences with people who find him so charming that they never demand to see the prince. You know, he is charming, but where is Prince Charming? And I think this has been the great emptiness in your life. You have been so pleasantly agreeable and acceptable, meeting everyone the way they want you to meet them, but you have never looked to the source of your charm and found the Prince.

>Steve: I find it so difficult not to be for people what they want me to be. Is there anything in particular that I can watch for in order to avoid that as much as possible?

Yes. Practise setting yourself in consciousness before you leave your room in the morning. Practise seeing the chair, for instance. Make it very simple. Practise seeing the *idea* of comfort appearing as a chair and fall not for the assumption that the chair, as a thing, is comfortable. Don't forget how the chair appeared: primarily as an idea in consciousness, secondarily as a thing. When you see this clearly, you can then go out and view your action in the same way, and you will find that you can appear to be what other people want you to be while you always remain what you really are. You see, what happens with you is that you start off with a fine and comfortable position, being lazy and a little hazy in the morning when you get up, and you let that fog continue until about eight o'clock at night. Then you start to wake up, because you know that you'll be able to go right back to sleep in four or five hours. And you can't do it this way, you see. Stay awake and appear to dissipate the fog by walking through it. And the greatest fog that surrounds you is your thought-projected world and its inhabitants. Oh no, there's no easy way to give you the Truth on a silver platter, but the words may appear as apples of gold in pictures of silver, as the Book of Proverbs says, but *you* have to keep them polished.

> Steve: Just for the record, have you ever seen me in the afternoon?

No.

> Steve: It is a perfect description of my day that you gave!

Is that so?

> Steve: To everyone but myself I appear to be in a fog until, as you say, around eight o'clock. I know that I'm not exactly asleep, but not exactly awake.

Well, of course, as long as you can appear that way you don't have to fulfill any responsibilities, and of course that's why you like it so much, and that's why it is so nice to let your friends think you are still half asleep, because no one expects anything from a sleep-walker, because a sleep-walker should never be disturbed. A sleep-walker should always be gradually led back to bed until he awakens on time.

> Steve: You said that there were better ways of avoiding pressures.

Yes. The best way to avoid pressure is by being Divine! The pressure of your physicality is due to the all-empowered act of Being wholly Divine. And as one aptly put it: "It is the pressure of your Divinity that appears as the discomfort of your personality." So, I'm glad you've been moved and bothered—not nearly enough—but after tonight you will be! You'll never have quite the same sense of peace again. You will sort of be filled with thorns and burrs; you'll never be able to be too comfortable after tonight. And this will be very good for you, because every time you start to wake up in a fog, you'll say, "Oh, Lord, I met this man and he saw right through my veils, and I have to see that I have to be on duty constantly." And others will say, "He neither moves to the east nor to the west nor to the north nor to the south, but stays fixed on That Spot and finds his base so comfortable as the Missile of Love has traced its path across the accomplishment of his Mountain." The Mountaintop experience awaits every man, but you can't go to the top of the Mountain and expect to go down and pull the old foundations of valley life up with you. That would be like trying to scale your structure of awareness while taking with you the weight of the blocks upon which it has been built. The Stone that the builders rejected has become the first stone or the cornerstone of your own temple. When those stones (or those truths) are literally taken, they can appear objectified (as churches, temples, synagogues, etc.), but when psychologically taken, they appear transparent.

> As the sands of the desert grow cold at night,
> And the winds howl in their lonely flight,
> You catch the power of the Omnipotent Sound,
> And know the howl of the Wind around
> Is only telling of That Event
> When all that is must seem so spent.
>
> Upon the arising of the Sun in the day
> You can look through the fog, for there the Ray
> Is penetrating by simply being at hand,
> Bombing the place of those who are dammed
> By beliefs and thoughts, which have only to bind
> And free not the heartstrings beyond the mind.
>
> And when you find that you have caught the pitch,
> Every string will come under tension in order to be pitched.
> And then in the act of acquiescing to Light,
> You tighten your strings—no loose ones in sight.
>
> And then, when the Conductor with Baton in hand
> Appears to give the upbeat for man,
> You can be sitting as one of the band

Saying, "Ah! Thank God I practised and I have been chosen to
    be part of the Symphony as planned."

So the university can only point
To the Universe beyond all thought,
For when you come to, you will find, no doubt,
That the degrees of accomplishment appeared because the Sun
    was said to be out.

And then when the cap is placed as planned
You'll say, "Ah, in the program and the recapitulation of Man
(The theme of Being at One, no doubt,
With the Principle of All), I AM found within, not without."

And within this power I can see my lot,
And you find it in your lap, and there's no believing it or not,
For the lot of your action has been cast as planned,
And the Missile of Love came on demand.

It was launched from the pad where the writing took place
With the pen so ready that a line could be traced
And given to men who would kick up some dust;
But by finding the linen was prepared, as it must
Be ever ready at hand and be sprayed, no doubt,
With the power to erase all dust about. [9]

You'll see that the table is laid in time,
Pointing to the Substance beyond the mind.
So take, eat, and drink of this Bread and this Wine,
And you'll see how the fish jumped at the Line Divine.
The Fish [10] always points without shadow of doubt
To Being One, which came from the School about.

And so you can say that the Line was cast
And the bait was Light, and you took it fast.
And then the act is forever One:
You're caught in the net and are in the Boat of the Sun.
So, with your Pilot may you direct your course
With no "Can you?" or "Will you?" but "I will do, of course."

---

[9] "Endust"... end of dust.

[10] Symbol of the Christ.

So, this is the end, or is it the beginning? No doubt!
Did you lose for a moment what the sound was about?
And if you did, that's how the Monolith came to be,
And when recognized, it was cast into the Light, you see
    [U.C.].

The Universal Christ is that mighty Power
That shakes every veil and rends those of the Temple of their
    power.
So, if you would be a priest unto the Self, there is no doubt;
You've got to be up on your toes, and they'll say, "Oh, you're
    certainly raising dust about!"[11]

What a windmill turned when the wind did blow
And you found you no longer stood where it was cold.

Oh, I wish we were here longer, Steve, for you to hear what
    I've said,
Because upon rehearing the tape, you will be quite surprised at
    what you thought I said.
Upon rehearing you will see that what you thought I said I did
    not say,
And upon seeing this, you will know how these words are
    arrayed.

Wouldn't you swear they were all just words?

> Steve: I can tell that they're not. I know that some of them seem just to go right by, so I know they're going someplace else.

The words that you hold onto are the words that mark the course of those that went to the point.

> Steve: It blew me away when you said in the poem, "This is the end," and the refrigerator stopped.

---

[11] "Raising dust about": agitating people's materialistic beliefs and opinions.

Well, it can often appear this way, and some of the new people who have come to see me in Toronto, and who have witnessed some of the amazing synchronicity that often occurs have said, "It was all contrived. Those things just happened because he planned it."

Steve: Maybe I was mistaking it for the refrigerator all the time—it wouldn't matter, though—but I think that you are humming that Pitch, the one that the Monolith gives off, all the time.

Jerry J.: I was hearing it also. I believe it was some mechanism over here, but I'm not sure.

Well, you hadn't better be! If you think it's in a thing, you will never have it, call it a refrigerator or what have you!

For That Which IS can appear as a tone,
For the T stands for Truth, and the O-N-E for One alone.
Tone.

When you're on pitch you can always tell when others aren't. But that doesn't mean that it should bother you, unless they want to play music with you. And if they do, they have got to be pitched correctly. Otherwise you will all sound like individualities ailing in time! The act of performance is to be superfluous and yet appear and have the act one of unification.

You can see the individuality of what appears as those in a quartet or a quintet or an octet, but the experience of the music is a unity. After a performance, one often hears comments on how fine the performers were. Yet, this can sometimes be a deceptive tribute, because it becomes evident that the performers stood out more than the music did! The performers should never stand out in the way that the music should be gowned. If this happens, then the individualities of the performers do not integrate into the common praise of music, and we often call this a personal accomplishment, as opposed to an inspired musical performance. The reason that a person stands out as being very fine in a group is often because the others aren't as fine. I remember hearing a performance of the Trout Quintet by Schubert, and I shall never forget it, it was so beautiful. But I didn't feel that it was primarily the performers that made it so beautiful. It was because they weren't in it personally that made the performance so beautiful. And yet, the performers appeared to be there, and so were we, and we were all very grateful that it was such beautiful music!

It's such a blessing, you see, when this happens; no one gets caught in the web of being a medium for music. Music is! The great difference today with composers is that many of them *work to write music* instead of dying to the suggestion that they could ever touch it, let alone write it! The only reason you write notes on a piece of paper is to prove to the mind that something has happened when it has died to time. And when you've finished you can say, "Ah, I've written all this music." No, you haven't. All you've written are a lot of black dots, but what you may experience will be something called a musical happening, and when it is experienced, some may say, "Oh, what a treat!"

It's somewhat like the light you see from this lamp. The light rays, which you say you see, are actually being reflected by the dust particles. You actually see the dust particles, but the dust particles are not the light. Similarly, the individual notes of a musical composition do not constitute the music. This light is only a counterfeit light. The Light That IS cannot be limited or defined, but can only be pointed to and remains, in essence, undefined. The Limitless can't be defined, but yet can be pointed to by the defined.

When sound is uncontaminated by personal involvement, it can bear healing. That's why you develop and practise technique, abstract exercises to build technique, so that no technical passage, no leap, is going to get in the way.

> Jaan: So, then all thoughts about having concern whether you can do it or not do it don't get in.

That's right. They don't enter into the performance. In this way you appear to die to your personal involvement and find yourself . . . not in the way.

> Steve: Earlene almost said that very thing last night. She was talking about her singing and how she feels it flows through her.

Yes, but a problem arises in that. You see, when people think that something is flowing through them, they are in the position of being divided. It is this very division that can cause upset in a person's life.

Steve: Yes, it is, but I don't think my intellect is realizing . . .

Well, your intellect can't "realize." That's how you have limited yourself all these years. "Intellect" is only the name given to coordinated thought patterns equated to specific situations that only bear a semblance of authenticity or reality until confronted by a fact. And the fact, of course, is the Light. As we've seen with the electric lamp, the light is not in the bulb or in the dust particles, but appears to shine through the bulb. Similarly, the Light of Consciousness is not in the intellect. You might say the Light shines through the intellect, but the intellect cannot stand in the way of the Light. It merely appears to be used by the Light for those who haven't seen the Light.

Steve: Even when it thinks it functions independently, it is still being used by the Light?

Yes, but it's only limited in its use by your thoughts about it.

Steve: That's very reassuring.

It is. It is reassuring to you, and it is very revelatory, for in the feeling of being reassured is the knowingness I AM present. You'll never lose your I-dentity, but you'll never find it in a book. You will never find it in any man's words, for it is already all there is. It just seems limited in its efficacy at times because of your thoughts about Being. Instead, just Be and let the blocks fall!

You know, you can easily talk yourself into a heavy situation, but you must remember that it is the Light ever-present that enables a heavy situation to appear heavy for the fun of it. You love being heavy, you know. You love being heavy, you love having your intellect, and you love being unsure about what you are going to do, because in this way you can evade what you know you must do, evade what you know you must say, evade what you know you do embrace, and evade what you know is your responsible action, all because you think and call it "I know I think" . . . or "I think I know." Well, *you* don't know; you think. "I" know, and you limit it by calling it your thinking or my thinking.

You will be at a loss around me, I will tell you that, because I wouldn't believe a darn thing you would say; I only know what you do. You see, you have built such an incredible wall around yourself. This I have tried to tell you. You are sort of in between two spots, two levels—I don't know how to describe it; it's fascinating to watch it—you have a base (and you know you mustn't be base!) and you have an aim, but you don't want to hit the bull's eye. No one would ever think you were obstinate, but you are extremely bull-headed. But after all, you can always get the bull to go when you get the fire behind it!

Steve: Or the carrot in front.

Yes, for a rabbit to leap. Well, jump, grasshopper, jump. Leap! Well, I really must stop because it's getting late.

# Equality

*Equality
is a "Sound Garment."
Where is there inequality
in a chant of praise?*

# 14 Equality

August 19, 1976, Sun-Scape Inn, Sparrow Lake, Ontario

This is the evening of August 19, 1976, and we are considering the nature and demands of equality. Equality is a state that the human race has deemed admirable, but it has never succeeded in experiencing it. It is a state of conscious attunement to the simplicity of Being. The simplicity of Being seems difficult to comprehend within the mayhem of the mind. The mind, in its attempt to usurp the Throne of the Almighty, has caused people to shine only partially. Also, many have not seen how the Light, even through the dark glass, does shine. Consequently, limits have encompassed them.

In the moment of inequality's recognition, disquietude came into the human race because the race was no longer realized as One. It was divided by the thoughts of Simplicity being complex, divided. Equality only exists as a desired dream among the complex situations of human being. Equality is never found among people; it is the garment of Individuality. But Individuality is not found in the framework of personality. Individuality has its roots in the indefinable and ultimate state of Indivisibility.[1] In the realm of Indivisibility, the only experience is the revelling of Oneness. Oneness means nothing to twoness, for twoness sees Oneness as a dream, whereas Oneness awakens the dreamer.

Equality is a "Sound garment." Where is there inequality in a chant of praise? The response to Sound [i.e., the authentic Spoken Word] is Sound response, the cure to the lack of acknowledgment, which is the first plague of the Age. To consider yourself as "another" is the root of inequality. To consider "another" is lack. To consider "another" in the Light of the Self is the root of equality. To consider your performance is an educational experience. To perform and then to be considered is an advanced step. Equality is not found in considering "another." Equality is the blessing that enables what appears as another to be found acceptable. Equality is bathed in wonder. The gift of wonder is the feeling of being equal in the Light of Self-realization. If I AM All, who is there besides My Allness? But to try to make "another" equal

---

[1] The root of the word "individual" is from the Latin *individuus,* which means "indivisible."

in "My Allness" is the attempt of the finite to accomplish in the name of the Infinite One.

Now, may you perceive that your perception bears a garment commensurate with the degree of your realization beyond your thoughts of being equal or unequal in the Light called I AM. I AM That I AM is your example of perfect equality. There is none other. Being I AM, your act of Soul enables *you* to appear in the same vehicle of cognition. The great verb "to be" has no need of an object, and yet ever fulfills itself in act, involuntarily. Not to act brings the lack of simplicity to the forefront, and in its place stands complexity, claiming attention. Simplicity shines with no reflective light.

Simplicity, a Light all its own, has no need of a reflector, but complexity is bound to one. To be simple is to be free; to be complex is to be bound. To experience the Nature of Being enables you to be born free. In the freedom of Being, I AM That I AM.

May these few words, which have come unto your range of conscious attention, so hold you in their embrace that you will find the embrace simply Sound. Others who know not a Sound embrace may say, "Equality unfurled its wings and only the Body of Sound [i.e., the Spoken Word] was present in the happening."

## How Do You Do?

*The only mistake
you have made is to think
there is some other action happening
other than That,
which is termed "I DO"!*

## 15     How Do You Do?

February 26, 1977, Arinaka, Tucson, Arizona

I want to start at eight-thirty on the button. What time is it? Two minutes to go. I would like to use this opportunity to say:

In the quickening of the Spirit, may you find in joy divine
How I am graced with finding you within my vision in time.
And may I offer thanks to you for all you've said and done
In offering in gratitude these gifts unto one.

I thank you in the meaning, freed from symbols when they're found,
And may you find what I mean when I say, "My thanks abound."
May you find it gathered unto that Point in Light,
Where you know the joy of receiving is all because you had what you gave to Light.

You know without a shadow that you can only give what you have,
And this is why I thank you, for I can only receive what I have.[1]
This is how I come to say I thank you all, who know
The joy of standing filled with wonder as the pageant of time appears to unfold.

This is the evening of February 26, 1977, which finds us in Tucson, Arizona, in the room that is called the one facing west. It is the room from which this greeting unfolds to all those who receive it in centres known and yet unknown and yet foretold. You who will hear this in Toronto, know that you are in the "gathering place," which is what Toronto has been called, and which is what this Indian word means. Regardless of what city you are in, you have brought upon yourselves your own life situations. You cannot blame it upon time. It is in time that you are found, it is on time that you will be seen, and it is in the seeing that you realize that you do not make over the old, but

---

[1] In order to receive a gift, one has to recognize it. The recognition itself indicates that the person already possesses an inner understanding and grasp of the gift offered, and in this sense receives what he already has.

drop it in appreciation of the new. Thus, all incapacities are seen to be swallowed up in the limitless possibilities of being found satisfied in the likeness of the Divine Ideal.[2]

You are spoken to because "I" is embracing the nature. You are spoken to and you will hear according to how you adore the "I" of embrace. Some of you who have come from here, there, and everywhere have come not knowing why. Some have come and only wonder. "Why" never entered their coming. Wonder fills their vision.

Remember, the language that I use in an Unfoldment is not personally oriented to your whims. An Unfoldment is given in such a way that the mundane is there, but is not given any undue attention. To transcend the limits of the mundane, you must fly as does the eagle above the suggested contaminated atmosphere of limits. If you are inclined to gain a new point of experience, you cannot gain it from an old point of inclusion. If you include an old point and expect to find a new one, you have to be willing to drop the old point, which often requires being jabbed by the new one!

If you are looking to find the point new, it is because you are fed up with the point old. You are where you are. If you are happy where you are, *Be* where you are. But if you are not happy where you are, it is obvious you are not *Being* where you are. It has been stated: "When God shines in the heart, it appears as a smile upon your face." In ancient times, these little statements of significance were called proverbs because they bore a point, especially when you didn't want to get it!

If you are to consider what you are doing here, then stop trying to consider what you are doing here from your not-doing here![3] You will never find what you are doing here if you do not find the Source from which you do. And you can never find the Source from which you do if you are completely inundated with *what* you do and not "*How* do I do?" When you meet somebody who says, "How do you do?" you naturally will say, "Stand in awe." And when someone says, "I beg your pardon?" say, "Do not beg my pardon, but beg that you hear what is stated, for there is no need for pardon, for the only mistake you have made is to think there is some action happening other than That, which is termed 'I DO'!"

---

[2] "Incapacities" became a theme of this Unfoldment because a man was present who had been crippled much of his life from polio.

[3] It is very misleading and in some cases harmful to make judgments before actually getting involved.

It is when you are concerned over what you do that you only partially do. You then ask "How do you do?" partially. When someone asks, "How do you do?" he may be asking because he is wondering either at your accomplishment or wondering why something hasn't been accomplished. So, when you are greeted with "How do you do?" just stop all thought and consider the tone of the voice that asked. It may not be a tone of greeting at all, but one that is pointing to whether or not your act has been given to and left in the lap of the Giver of every good and perfect gift. If you are only concerned about what you do, you are forgetting the Doer, which is not "you." Yet, because the Doer is All-inclusive in nature, "you" appear to do, and may it be termed, "Well done, thou good and faithful servant." In this understanding, may you inherit the full recognition of work well done, which points to the periphery of that state of Consciousness called the Kingdom of Heaven.

The reason you are aware of incapacities is that incapacities go with earth. The reason you are dissatisfied with apparent incapacity is that you know innately that your capacity to Be is unlimited. It is every man's birthright, because every man has Consciousness reigning, despite his thoughts about it and despite his gigantic or dwarfed states of cognition, evident in his varied garments of personality. Remember, when you are found present in the world, you must also find yourself present in Heaven so that the world may be freed from being what it isn't.

Some have tried to engage many levels of action in order to understand how they act and move. However, if they had stopped to consider *how* they really act and move, they might have rescinded the necessity of taking action other than that of God-Being. God-Being is not limited, save by thought, and God-Being is not "you." God-Being is the Light to "you." The sunbeam is not the sun, but separate them if you can. When you say you see one, there's bound to be the other.

If you go around thinking you are God, you bear the burden of supporting His creation. You are also taking a long time in your walk through the garden of earth. After all, God did it and it was done! It is suggested in the Esoteric Teachings that when you once see That Which IS, all laws that would seem to bind you to that which isn't are rescinded. The eagle may partake of the food of the mundane level, but its flight far transcends the plane of limits. It engages such height that undoubtedly from its high point of observation you appear as nothing but a tasty mortal—morsel!

If you would fly, you cannot be concerned about your weighty situation. Flight suggests buoyancy, and buoyancy suggests that weight [i.e., attachment to the mundane] is incidental. Weight enters the picture because of your thoughts and because of your lack of an ideal. If you are to move beyond incapacity, you must take an ideal and claim it. That will lead you into a new way of viewing.

It appears that many people feel that the mind must give its consent before they can appropriate those thoughts that point to the delineation of an ideal. An ideal points to a new state. Your mind is the only thing that you have bred (by constantly feeding it erroneously) that stands in the way of the Actual State. You see, when you are not thinking about what you are not, all that's left over is what you are! But erroneous thinking[4] takes you right back into Karma.[5] And yet, Karma is the only thing that the mind has to offer you as hope.[6] But what hope is there for you if you know you're deliberately taking an erroneous point of view? How do you expect to be freed from it unless you knowingly drop it? If you take it, you can drop it. But so many take it and persist in holding onto it because they persist in being what they are not, and yet, they are so dissatisfied with their incomplete, unsatisfied, and unfulfilled life actions.

The reason people move from one place to another is that they say the move offers opportunity. The only thing about opportunity is that if you are going to enter its sphere, you have to be ready to accept it. Opportunity doesn't say, "I want you where you are"; opportunity says, "I want you for being capable of meeting my demands, which points to a door opening, for when I stand at the door and knock, you have the possibilities open to you of entering into a new state of Consciousness." And when you find you do have this opportunity, you continue to be what you seem to be [i.e., human], but you are not knotted in it, because of what you know.

When you *think* you know, you are "knotty." When you know you know, you may appear to think, but you are able to point to the Wisdom that transcends the wisdom of time. This points to the gift that comes when intuition speaks and your mind of thoughts is silenced. It is then that you

---

[4] Thinking from a personal standpoint rather than from the standpoint of God.

[5] From the author's first book, *Given to Praise!* (Toronto: Sun-Scape Publications, 1976), p. 135: "Karma is not what you get for doing something wrong, it's what you get for not being what you are."

[6] The hope is that one will be freed from his limits when he has worked through their Karmic effects.

perceive the message of what is termed a God-like communication. You cannot have thoughts about intuition, because intuition transcends thought. It is intuition that enables the Divine Ideal to be delineated by thoughts. An ideal points to the new, but so often is misrepresented by incorrect language. That is why you have to recognize and utilize Principle, the unshakeable Point. Otherwise you get caught in the incorrect statements that so many give. You must always strive to point to the Ideal that is beyond all mistake.

An ideal doesn't have a mistaken identity; only "you" do! An ideal always points to something new, and that something new must conform to what you term to be the goal, the purpose, and the aim of your life. If you're going to be a ditch digger, may you be the finest ditch digger; if you're going to be a gold digger, be the finest gold digger, but don't be taken by one who wants to dig for *your* gold [i.e., anyone who tries to use you]. If you're going to be a businessman, be about the business as the Father would be about His business. If you are going to be a musician, get out of the way so that music may say, "You have practised well, and my melody encompasses all who hear it and who free it from the limits of being just an earthly round." If you want to be a dancer, by all means, dance, and appear to dance with someone else if necessary, knowing that God is the Source of the rhythm, for rhythm prepares the intuitive leap right into His lap.

When you dance, you expect flexibility. You do not conceive of a dancer being unable to bend. I would ask how many of you are mentally entertaining the idea of dancing with me [i.e., moving in rhythm with the Unfoldment and its steps]? If you ever entertain it, start practising flexibility. There is nothing more rewarding than to bow to wonder. There is nothing more energizing than to give praise when prayer has been answered. There is nothing more sustaining than the experience of a Pitch that enables all those who love to find Life full of meaning as Love embraces the act.

We all talk about love but leave it subject to our thoughts because we all have our ideas about love. The reason you find love not fulfilling is that you are still dwelling in the realm where capacity is limited. Love never claimed a position that was subject to limits. The reason you find love changeable is that you think in the framework that says love has to do with a thought that inflates your deflated sense of being embraced. But Love is the Power that can cause your mind, upon giving its consent, to be found at the altar before it is ever published before the congregation of time. Love enables the Wedding [i.e., Mystical Union; marriage of head and Heart] to take place so rapidly that there is no way to ask, "Who is there present who would declare that this situation should not take place?" When I was married, I saw through the false suggestion that I could ever be divorced from what I AM, and as a result, my idea of marriage took a new leap. Only then was I able to see marriage as a genuine approach to Union.

It is one thing to have your heart ever-faithful; it is another thing to find the head bowing to the Heart full of meaning. The head is constantly the cup of change. You perhaps already know the great symbology surrounding the Chalice: it was the embodiment of the great search that a great king offered[7] from the plane beyond limits to all those who could bear the ability to interpret the esoteric messages surrounding the initiations into the higher echelons of awareness and still appear to meet a lady in distress.[8] Now, those knights of such a round table claimed a Figure seen [i.e., a Christ figure or Ideal], but knew that such a Power could never be left in the changing picture of time. The Custodian of all Wisdom is not in person, but is found in and as the ever-flowing Stream of Newness borne on the wave of submission. You cannot enter into the Stream of everlasting Life, as it is sometimes called, by standing on the bank.

Now, some have said, "I have only a few dollars to invest." Some have said, "I have invested stock, but my broker was broke, and I have no stalk/stock with which to stroke across this river [of living] in order to get off this bank. I had better stay and hold this stance." Where is your flexibility? *Dive* into the Stream and see if the Breath of God will not keep your head a'bobbing above the water until the head is robbed of its suggestive power to keep you afloat. It is in the buoyancy of Life that the weightiness of body seems to be carried on the tide of the Eternal Truths.

It is one thing to speak; it is another thing to see it written. You will find that there is nothing new being said when you read enough, but it is interesting to find it being said before it is read! To treat the mind to a cup of rejoicing enables the mind to be filled with the wine of inspiration. But if you do not hold such opportunity, which affords itself as joy ever at hand, then you will find your cup emptied by those who would claim your joy but give nothing up or nothing back in taking it. They submit not to the act that is garmented in joy. They say instead, "What right have you to be joyous, when I am filled with my own conceit? I am so dissatisfied that I cannot bear you joyous!" And you say, "Oh, but you know that is not true. You are the image

---

[7] The Chalice referred to is the Holy Grail, for which King Arthur searched.

[8] Referring to the feminine aspect of consciousness, the intuitive, emotional, receptive phase, which is always in "danger" of being repressed by the rational, aggressive, masculine phase.

and likeness of God, and if you would only just look here or there, you might see what it is to be happy, wealthy, and wise. You don't need to be like so many who stand on the bank, always causing the country to be taxed." And before too many days have passed, you find that you, in your joy that is full and evidenced by exalting, are now only moved to say, "Well, I know that your lack of joy isn't true, and if I had time, I would sit down at the table and try to help you see through the mind's propaganda about what you aren't." Leave your acts of mercy in the garment of joy and forget whether or not they are creating an impression.

  If you are going to try to impress someone, remember, you must first of all be thinking of yourself as an impression. If you are making an impression, you must be in that which is made. You are, therefore, subjecting yourself needlessly to the limits of the three dimensions. But if you are offering a Sound experience [i.e., offering thought, word, and deed spontaneously from the higher Standpoint], then you are the evidence, just in the attitude of joy and all-inclusiveness, of the power and the glory right on the plane of earth. You find you are able to offer to others the opportunity of entering the ever-new state of Consciousness, which is above the limits of earth and its incapacity and is termed the Kingdom of Heaven or the realm of Infinite Opportunity.

  Opportunity knocks once, they say, on earth. But I feel opportunity is forever present when Heaven is freed from the limits of being a place to go when you die. It is the grace that descends when you free yourselves consciously from being the children of lies and the future fathers of them. You will probably not be popular if you stand for what you know to be true. But after all, if you know what is true, you must *be* what is true. As a result, the only stand is what others say you take as you live.

  Your living should be an inspiration to those who are the living dead. Earth is another name for the life process in decline. Heaven is that state of Consciousness which knows nothing but the momentous Now. You can say, "Oh, yes, I can think my way into that." You may find that you already have, because after all, if your mind has given consent to your entering it, then your mind must have already appeared before the Altar of the Light. The benediction is there: "Whom God hath joined together, who is there on earth to put it asunder?"

  If you pay for a choir of angels to chant while you are signing the register and putting a sign on a piece of paper that you've done it, you know very well that the time will come when you will have to pay for believing that

"I" could ever have been in a divided state! I AM fully satisfied when I AM seen in the Light of Love. People may say, "What would happen, Mr. Mills, if people didn't marry?" Don't pay any attention to such a question. Just ask them to dream up their own answers when they sleep.[9] In fact, the reason some people sleep so much is to get away from the suggestion that there is such a state![10] You see, it was never meant that *two* should *try* to live together. It was meant that in Love there is only *One* living and moving and having Being.

      A gold ring acknowledges the marriage union. To Michael G. it was said earlier this evening that in the age of silver, all men were tied to their mothers and were often quarrelsome and moody. Just take a look at the world today and see if we have really left the silver age in order to enter the New Age of Gold.

      You who have been present with me during this week of considering beauty have hopefully come to see how you sometimes mar it by not knowing that you cannot touch beauty with a point of thought that is not one with it. All you need to do is look at it and it may entice you to consider well its grace. If you have looked into the sound of the Unfoldments, upon second or third hearing you have perhaps perceived that what you thought you were hearing had little relevance to what was actually said. And yet you would still presume to know. It is much better not to presume to know, but to Be.

      To Be is like a match. A match left in a box holds a promise that when struck correctly, it may be freed from its catatonic state. A match struck by the Light is said to have a flaming head, which can set others aglow. If it is too hot to handle, it is often well to use some form of insulation so that you will not get burned if you are not one with it. Sometimes it is suggested that you dunk the "match" in water to cool it off before you dare to handle it. I tell you now, the whole purpose of the Flame is not to destroy, but to free.

      A box containing a match could be like a room in the dark. But when you take courage and refuse to be intimidated by a crystallized chemicalization [i.e., like the match-head], you may find that when you have been struck correctly, your head is filled with Light. What you previously thought was a chemical situation that caused you to react has now given you an act of

---

[9] The point being made is that such considerations fade out in the sleep state, thus showing their impermanent and limited value.

[10] Those who are unhappily married may use sleep as their first avenue of escape.

such transcendency that you are able to see right into the very room that was dark, which you had hitherto not even considered looking at [i.e., the subconscious], for after all, it was buried under the ashes of dark belief.

The reason words are used in the Unfoldment is that *you* have used them. The reason words can be used to free you from them is that there is only One, which is free of you. "You" came about, it is said in the Esoteric Teachings, when you went to sleep in the garden. Upon awakening, you found a tree and a fruit. Remember, you were told that you were not to partake of the fruit if you did not want to know of good and evil. But in sleep, in ignorance, when you forget what IS, you enter onto the plane of choice. The plane of choice is what has trapped so many. Yet, when I AM All, where is there choice?

Remember, the apple couldn't have come about if there hadn't been the root of tree, the bud, the blossom, and the fragrance. If you have ever been in an apple orchard in blossom time, you have undoubtedly been filled with wonder at the blossoms and have been intoxicated with their fragrance. Then, in knowing the opportunity that was awaiting when the blossom faded, you were prepared to partake of the result of the blossom's dying to your sight: its down-to-earth body called an apple. If you were not insensitive, you realized that the fragrance had become the flavour.

It all happened because a seed was planted and you doubted it not. Then you found by having planted one seed, the apple contained within itself not only the promise of its essence, the fragrance, but also the possibility [opportunity] of another entire orchard. The Core of Being is forever wrapped in the Seed of Truth. It only waits to be planted in fertile soil prepared by one who is dissatisfied with experience as it seems to be, who is prepared to give consent to Experience as it IS, and who awaits the great Gardener of Cosmic Light.

You see, no one knows how a seed is planted, but it is said that when the time is right and two come together, the result is termed another of your own kind. It is so interesting that you never doubt that you will have one of your own kind, but yet you are filled with doubt about the Seed that is planted as Truth bearing Truth, not after *your* own kind, but after the image and likeness of the Effulgence that is the Light unto your earth of limits, which opens the gates into that state of Consciousness that is termed Heavenly. Heaven is not some place you will go to when you die. Heaven is that state of Consciousness that is present now, but misunderstood by being thought of in terms of earth.

Bend your knee and knock, for as Jesus said, "Love one another as I have loved you." I would say, "Exalt one another as I have exalted One to you."

## "I Have Overcome the World"

*In overcoming the world,
may you overcome the limits
of form and be found levitated
to your rightful place
in the Kingdom of Realization.*

## 16    "I Have Overcome the World"

October 7, 1978, Sun-Scape Inn, Sparrow Lake, Ontario

This is the afternoon of October 7, 1978, and we find ourselves beside the hearth at a place that is located in a retreat near the Centre [i.e., Sun/Son-Scape Inn] in which the Will shall be known. We find ourselves congregated on the rim or on the edge of that lake where the sparrow is always held in remembrance of the Divine Mother. We find ourselves here in the gown of an autumn cavalcade of power, and we find ourselves adorned by the "decking" appearing as a scaffold of such power.[1] The world is said to be in need of such a structure raised beyond the confines of the mind and supported by a contrite, expectant, and versatile heart-responsiveness.

We are moved, as never before, due to our place on the calendar of events, to consider the great exigencies surrounding the speculatory situations of time. It is well that we have come to meet, you might say, in this announced conclave, in order that those who are present may assemble, with even more ability and agility, the innately acquired gifts that are waiting to be called forth into the action of those who would be in the vanguard of the parade of Stars, and who would be carrying the banner of the Masters of Wisdom.[2]

You who have considered what you are doing here as a result of such questions popping to the mind as: "Is what I am doing worth doing?" and "What am I doing here?" are becoming more and more aware of what your purpose is as you are entering and finding yourselves stationed at a place of importance in the experience called living at this time. You are here

---

[1] Mr. Mills refers to the colours of the autumn trees in their "decking" as being a "scaffold." The scaffold is a symbol that suggests the availability of the many levels of meaning that can be seen and experienced, even in coloured leaves, as one considers more than the literal. In the study of metaphysics, symbols themselves are often like a scaffold in that they enable a structure of experience to be raised.

[2] The "innately acquired gifts" refers to qualities such as devotion, compassion, understanding, intuition, etc., all of which are required of the serious spiritual aspirant. The "parade of Stars" refers to the appearance of the great and acknowledged spiritual Masters of all Ages.

for a much greater purpose than you think, because as you know, it doesn't take time to think right. If you are able to view "it doesn't take time to think right" correctly, you will find yourself rescinding the superstition surrounding "time-thinking." Time-thinking goes with human thinking; Divine Consciousness embraces conscious, spiritual attainment.

What is the purpose of our place in the world when we know we are not just human? What is the place going to do with us, and what are we going to do with the place? The purpose of our being is to bring to this plane, for those who are on it in trance, the experience of coming face to face with what is termed a different state of consciousness, sometimes called a spiritual consciousness. This spiritual consciousness is really a higher state of the mental realm, but it is not as inundated with the weight of the dross body — rather, the *gross* body and its considerations. The dross is what we lose involuntarily by gaining the spiritual consciousness, even while appearing to be mentally engaged in pursuing, subduing, and appropriating the demands of intellectual constructs.[3]

We are here not to put an end to intellectual accomplishment; we are here only to see that the intellectual accomplishment is propagating the Child of the spiritual seeding. Spiritual seeds are planted in the husks of ideas. Ideas buried in fertile soil take root and burst forth into a form befitting their nature. In other words, you would not plant the seed of a tree and expect a marigold! The seed carries within it the blueprint that has outlined what the tree or the flower shall be. Similarly, the Divine Idea that you contain, when planted and nurtured amid the ideas of the Teaching, brings forth what your tree, what your flower, what your blossom, what your stalk, shall be. It is not to be planted and then looked at, because you would never expect to have a tree grow if you uncover the seed after it has started to germinate and say, "What is the matter with you? I can't sit in your shade yet!" You know that in the Light it doesn't take time, but it does take persistence and practise to hold the Divine Accomplishment as a realization termed "Christ Consciousness." You must sustain this sense of persistence, because if you don't, you will not be able to perceive the thrusts of the root, or the higher, spiritual stirrings, on the periphery of your lake of consciousness, which at the moment are happening beneath the realm of cognition. Yet, these stirrings are known, because the doors of perception have opened to those who have walked through the pages of time and who have held aloft a Message of Transcendency. The Message could never have been held before the intellect of any time if some

---

[3] Pointing to "being in the world but not of it." "Dross" refers to beliefs not founded on fact.

portion of the intellect were not timed. Yet, there is some portion of the intellect that is timeless, and that is why the intellect will never be in a situation in which it will be exterminated. Instead, it will be offered the seed of rejuvenation, for it will hold within your consciousness the promise of what it is to be part of the entourage of Light.

You see, if we are thinking in terms, we are thinking as humans. The "terms" (social customs, morals, etc.) should always be present as guidelines under which we operate, but the "terms" should only be there as guidelines until our intellects are no longer inundated with the spurious data that has sprung into existence as a result of false reasoning. The Sight that sees no terms is founded on the Rock of Understanding, which is known to be a constant. There is no conditioned Being; Being is unconditional. It doesn't take time to think right; it only seems to take time for you to come to see that your experience is not necessarily limited to your incarnation as a human. It only seems limited to your incarnation as a human as long as you think through the framework of a computered thought structure and forget that you too are actually capable of saying, "The doors of perception have opened, and I perceive I AM Conscious Being, and as a gift for those in time, appear to carry a mentality struck by the Light!"

Now, as we approach this incredible time, we have to bring into consideration what makes this time so unusual. You could say it has to do with you and me being present. That is so, but there is no value of you and me being present if you and me persist in being "you" and "me." The only value of you and me being present is that we carry the Present of Promise. The Present of Promise is the living Presence of That, which has been offered unto all men who seek the Self All-glorious.

Jesus said, "Be of good cheer; I have overcome the world."[4] What does this simple statement mean? It has gone into theological avenues, fine and dandy, but I would wonder if theologians have ever considered that Jesus's accomplishment rested in the simple experience of considering "How do I see?" "Be of good cheer, for I have overcome the world." Jesus may well have been saying, "If you watch me, more than chewing over my words, you might see how 'I' have overcome the world." How do you see? How do we see? How we see and how you see is the value of us. There is no possible way to overcome the world as it seems to be. We have to consider so carefully how we see. We take it so casually. If I say, "A pencil is for sale," what kind of pencil would you like to see for sale?

---

[4] John 16:33.

Michael G.: One with an eraser and "HB" lead.

What kind of pencil would you like to see for sale?

Joelle M.: One that would make my writing very legible, and one that has a hard lead.

Yes.

Mary C.: A lead pencil.

Christopher D.: I would like to have a gold one.

You see, there is nothing wrong with any of them, and there is nothing right with any of them. But look how differently you see them! I just said "a pencil," but each one thought of the pencil in his own way, and that is why you must have something in common to hold your thought to so that you will all be thinking about the same thing! We have all got to come to point. A pencil has to be fashioned for use, and that is done first by the manner in which you see it.

Now, when I say, "Mind can be changed," what do I mean?

Judy O.: The images that are held can be refined.

Yes, Ted?

Theodore H.: Thoughts can be molded.

Gurcharan?

Gurcharan S.: The ideas that constitute the mind can be changed.

Yes. Donna?

Donna C.: The thoughts can be changed.

Chris?

Christopher D.: To me, it means that I am more than mind.

Now, if we accept Chris's statement that "I am more than mind," it means that a mind that can be changed cannot be the Mind that IS. There is the key to being more than mind, because if you can change your mind, there must be a Mind that is greater that can change it! Now, the best way to change your mind is through changing your image, changing your ideas, watching your thoughts. That is how you appropriate the platform of an Experience on which you are more than mind.

Now, that Experience is only known by the careful utilization of words, which are used and sponsored by the intellect. Yet, the Experience points beyond the intellect. No one can give you that State, but when you arrive, it is known just like *that* because it is in no way affected by your thoughts about you or your thinking in time. Do not be afraid to dwell on timeless considerations.

If you have a problem, the only way to get rid of it is to do away with the belief that *Principle* could have a problem. You do not try to do away with *your* problem. All you do is rejoice in the known fact that Principle could not possibly be having a problem. You may seem to be going through one heck of a problem, but the fact is, it is truly not so. Now, you do not try to make you me.[5] In other words, the problem is "you and me." You do not solve your problem by making you me. You come to the solution of the conundrum by realizing that what enables you and me to consider a point (be it a problem or not) is a State that is beyond the mental limits of time. You see, what you are accomplishing here and now is what is opening you to the eternal Substance of Conscious Being, freed from the minimizing effects of personalization, humanization, or individualization.

The reason you are here is that the world has need of you, because you know not only the likes of me, but you also know me as you are as I AM. That is the point. You and I are important only in proportion to our ability to carry everything that is simply Divine, while still appearing to be what we appear to be. There is no reason under the sun that you are not the wealthiest, healthiest creatures on this plane. In reality, you are, regardless of what stones you may have, either on your fingers or in your heads! But do not forget to include the acknowledgment of elegance in your declarations every day when you awake. Elegance must be part of your declarations. Many of you evidence elegance and many of you are coming to evidence elegance. You must not only evidence elegance, but you must also evidence involuntarily

---

[5] Mr. Mills alerts his students against projecting their problems onto someone else, particularly him.

the grace that comes with it, because you cannot have elegance without grace. The greatest grace is to know you have received, and the greatest dividend is found in response.

One of the most ancient and deleterious sins known to men and women who are on the Path is lack of response. I read this recently. No wonder I am constantly concerned about lack of response! Every High Teaching tells you that when the intuitive response happens and you move on it, it automatically brings with it the need to be prepared to withstand resistance from your "friends." Remember, intuition is not mental. Intuition is that power, that grace, that glory that enables you to know that you have something beyond your mind, because the intuition functions beyond the mind level of consideration. Now we come to a very important point to perceive: it is this very ability of intuition to function in this manner that is such a fear to those who say, "It takes time to think it out." While you are thinking it out, intuition has already done it.

If you are of importance on this plane at this time, it is obvious that your importance is due to more than your ability to "think it out." You might say that being here with me goes hand in hand with an ability that you must start evidencing more and more. I am referring to the ability to perceive intuition speaking. Cease trying to think it out! Be very cautious, because as soon as intuition has spoken and you start to "think it out," you find you have a foreign language to deal with. You become confused. "Thinking it out" is completely foreign to intuition speaking. It is important to perceive this. On the other hand, you will find that if you always have to explain to others every move you make intuitively, you will need much patience, because it will take you an hour or more to explain how you have arrived at a certain point!

How do you see? [Mr. Mills holds up a box of matches, the cover of which is decorated with a flower print.] You say, "Ah yes, it's a box of matches." How do you know it is? This is it. *How* do you know it is? The next sin is assumption. The most ancient of sins is lack of response. The next sin is the sin of assumption.

You say this is a box of matches. It looks like a flower garden. You were looking at this thing and picturing it to be a box of matches. I was looking at it and seeing a flower garden. This is why you have to be so careful of what you say. You see, most of you think you are talking about a box of matches, while others are thinking of something inside, hoping they can strike it. Somebody else may be looking at it and wishing they had it, while another person may be saying, "Boy, what an idea for a garden." And you say you are considering a box of matches? We have no right to those considerations if we are speaking about overcoming the world! There is no room for speculation. Now, to overcome the limit called "the box of matches," the most basic thing you have to come to realize is what?

        Pamela L.: That the box of matches is a thought.

Yes, but what do you first recognize it to be?

        Pamela: A thing, an object.

It is an object. That is the word I wanted. Is the object always present?

        Pamela: No, sir.

That is the first step in starting to gain control. If this object is not always present, then you cannot give it the allegiance that you would to something that is always present. So, are you concerned if it is not always present?

        Students: No.

Why? You must know the answer to that question. Why?

        Joan P.: Because your allegiance belongs to That which is always present.

Which is . . .

        Hermine S.: Idea.

Yes, idea. You see, if you want a box of matches, you say, "I call for a box of matches." The idea is always beyond taking time to think right. The idea of the thing is always a conscious experience beyond the thing. That is why you can always have a box of matches, because the *idea* (which is the essence of the box of matches) is always capable of being called upon. But you do not try to preserve the box of matches. You always remember what a box of matches really is: the catatonic state of light. So, you do not mind using it up, for you are always striking the light, and the Light is limitless! So, you will always have a box of matches if you keep it as a Divine Idea.

Recognizing this fact, a box of matches becomes limitless for those who can entertain the *idea* of a box, wood, a chemical head, and an irritating surface (the last two of which dominate the mental experiences of most people today!). Look at how many of you "sticks" have got yourselves boxed into cartons of mentality and have found the thoughts that constitute it to be chemicalizing. For years you try to reason and rationalize your life experiences. You take all kinds of courses in psychology, all kinds of courses in higher abstract reasoning, yet you are not free of the basic issue of being boxed in by your thoughts. But then along comes the *idea.* You see, outward manifestation of the box is the limited expression of mentality, but the *idea is itself an expression of Consciousness.* The box is mental; the idea is conscious experience. When you can bring the two together and have an irritating surface—like me, and you rub against me [Mr. Mills takes a match from the box and strikes it], you are struck by the Light! You thought it was going to be so irritating, but your chemicalization soon disappears. You then turn into a flame and you transcend your whole body of limits. But tell me something, at the end [Mr. Mills blows out the match], the match may have disappeared, but has it? As an idea it lives. [He takes another match from the box.] Another wonder! It has a different appearance, but look. [He strikes the match.] The flame is exactly the same. It has a different appearance and everything else, but is the flame different?

Students: No, sir.

But if you had not called upon the Divine Idea, you would have gone around like those of your world, not knowing a means to an end as the beginning ... of Newness. Now, "Be of good cheer, for I have overcome the world." Be of good cheer; I have overcome the *objective beliefs of the world.* If you have overcome the objective beliefs of the world, what kind of a world do you really live in? Are you living in or on the world?

Students: Yes.

You appear to be, but are you always conscious of living in or on the world? Is the world always present? Is it there when you sleep?

Students: No.

But why is it present when you wake up in the morning? Because it is what?

Hermine S.: It is held as an idea.

It is a conscious experience. It is a conscious state, and it is sustained by your attention. Now, the third great sin is the lack of attention ... to

177

detail. You do not live on an arid planet. The detail is enormous in its infinitesimal perfection, from the grain of sand to the giant tree of the great sequoia forests to the giant stone monoliths of Monument Valley. It is perfect in every way. You see, God's work, as the Bible tells us, was perfectly done, and He was satisfied with it and termed it "good."

      Why are we giving thanks? Because we have inherited the legacy of being of good cheer because "I" have overcome the world. Thanksgiving for what? For the ability to perceive the legacy "'I' have overcome the world." You know, the reaping and harvesting of this Thanksgiving time has happened, to some degree, mentally. The "crops" [fruits of practice] have been harvested, the pickling has been done, all kinds of preserves have been made, the tomatoes are there, waiting for the wax caps to be affixed tightly to the bottles they are in. And you are wondering if they are going to make it through the winter months—ask Joyce. She has had so many pickling sessions and so many preserving sessions, and she knows that those caps have to be sealed correctly. Why was she concerned? Because if the wax seal broke on what had been prepared during the harvest, it would not be good to eat in the spring. If the seal is broken, it will not be good when you need it. Similarly, you cannot break the seal that has been affixed to what you claim as Real and expect to find it of any value when you need it. What you harvest as a result of your daily actions of living to the best of your ability from the standpoint of Principle, you are "preserving." But when you deny such a Principle and thus deny the Giver of every good and perfect gift, you are breaking the "Seal of Approval"[6]—and you will never be sponsored by "good housekeeping!" "Good housekeeping" is keeping in order what is necessary to satisfy the demands of the hearth. It is such a *magazine* of power,[7] because it becomes the Soul's fortification for the days when you are to offer your ability to appear in the world in the vanguard of an action that bears the banner of good cheer.

      How are you seeing? Are you seeing you and me being separate, or so greatly in love that What IS becomes a living force in our experience, causing the fields to appear suddenly ripe for harvest? There is so much in such a storehouse that must be shared with all those who call upon you in need. But remember, if you offer your personal thoughts to people who call upon you in need, you are offering them tainted food. How are you seeing?

---

[6] "This is my beloved Son in whom I am well pleased." See the author's cassette/transcription publication, *The Seal of Approval* (Toronto: Sun-Scape Publications, 1979).

[7] From the Old French *magazin*, storehouse.

Many people have written books on this, but for you, books on it should be unnecessary at this point. After hearing it stated so simply, you should have all that is necessary to look right through the realm of limits.

So, we have much to be thankful for. May you be open to the descent of God's Grace appearing as you being able to elucidate the principles surrounding your perceptions. May you be able to lead others to the doorway of the Light. This is what Thanksgiving is about. Thanksgiving is what you are about. You call Thanksgiving the season in which the earth gives to you what you have planted in it. But is it really this way? Are you sure you are seeing correctly? Perhaps *you* are what has been planted and are now present as the offering to the earth! On this the sun shines! You are seedlings in the forest of time. Time is made up of thoughts, but your Gift is thought-less. It is involuntarily bestowed, because "All that I have is thine" as conscious experience and harvest. You can only take into your storehouse what you have made room for by responsiveness, by attentiveness, and by your ability to appropriate. Never assume that you know when you are all bound up with you and your reasoning ability.

Your place on this planet, which is where you are perceived, is of paramount importance. I cannot tell you strongly enough that you have got to cease being such boxed instruments. But you should be the evidence of such containment that all would ask for what you have gleaned as a result of having attuned your hearts to the outpourings of Grace and attuned your heads to the Principle likened unto God, unto I AM That I AM. This Principle is found applicable and a living experience right where you are and as you are. In this understanding, we bring to this plane the opportunities of a World without end, for it has no beginning. Each day arises to be graced by your conscious attention to detail; each day sets so that you may glean what you have brought to your place in the sun.

On this is Thanksgiving predicated, on this awareness is life offered, and on this plane cheer dwells. Through the sheer veils that exist as a result of thoughts we look and find the landscape wearing the variegated garment of the Invisible Artist appearing formed. In having overcome the world, may you overcome the limits of form and be levitated to your rightful place in the Kingdom of Realization, in which Principle acknowledged becomes known as God for those who are willing to do so. Principle experienced without a name becomes Christ Consciousness, for which the world waits. In this present is wrapped the presence of Thanksgiving.

You and I appear graced to be living as the "universal solvent" to the situations of time. In this act, may we be found fructifying and magnifying the Light of all perception, the Source of all wonder, and the magnitude of "All that I have is given to praise." In this be satisfied, for in this, "I" am always about my Father's business, and in this is the Will being made known. It is stated that "I" must be glorified, because in Being, the garment is cheer, vitality, and energy. In Being is found the centre of attraction, and all filings and seedlings may have their systems realigned to the magnetic pole of wonder and grace, all wrapped up in a colourful leaf upon your autumn tree. A Way *is* found, and in this, rejoice.

# A Moment's Celebration as Easter

## The central, universal Factor of all faiths is Awareness.

## 17   A Moment's Celebration as Easter

March 11, 1979, Arinaka, Tucson, Arizona

This is Sunday evening, March 11, 1979, at Arinaka, Tucson, Arizona. We are finding ourselves, and in order to find any treasure, we have to know the fabled stories about where it is buried. Maps and charts have been given throughout the ages about the great mountains of gold hidden beneath the surface of recognition, hidden beneath the surface of that part of man's world that he thinks is out of sight. We who are forever in search of the richness of Being always know and are wary of the fact that as our perceptions increase in power, as they increase in beauty, they become objectified in beauty, tempting us to think that the treasure is where it is seen outwardly, where it is felt outwardly, and where it can be estimated in worth outwardly. We know so well that we perceive according to our state of awareness. We know that we perceive according to what we deem desirable within our natures and to how worthwhile we deem getting beyond the nature of desire and its limits.

Some say that they will share the wealth of a found treasure with the country in which it was found. Some say, "We will divy it up. We will divide it. We will naturally restore half of it to the source from which it came, and the other half we will keep to ourselves." That may be all right in the plans of time, but in the plans of the Kingdom of the Light, nothing can be kept from the Source from which it springs. Everything must return to the Source, for there is nothing that is apart from the Source, save that which is held in belief to be separated from the Source. We may not know of a chest of gold, but we do know that if we can be shown it and thus can *image* it, we can perceive the chest objectified, either filled or emptied of its treasure, all according to whether or not we desire the fullness commensurate with the state of completeness.

Desire enters into the picture on the level in which all men and women are found trying to bring together what constitutes meaningful events in their lives. Every event that you experience, every event that you find, is a result of an unspoken desire. What you desire will appear according to the demands and intensity of your desire. If you truly desire to be complete, then you will find yourself complete as I AM. Then the desire will not be left on the plane where you think "you" can be satisfied. The desire is satisfied, but you move to another plane where you know very well that to be satisfied is to find, not the desire fulfilled as you think, but fulfilled as you know, for true fulfillment springs within the very resources of your own Beingness.

You who have considered some aspects of your treasure hunt know very well that many maps are offered to the public, and many enticing yarns are spun about the great ships that have gone beneath the waves, bearing such treasures with them. But we also know that in the conscious realm of Being, there is nothing hidden that shall not be revealed. In order to find a thing revealed, we know very well that it all depends upon our effort and willingness to understand the situation not as it seems to be, but as it really is. We must always be filled with wonder at the riches and at the evidence of how perception, the power of imaging, and the power of will have brought us our just riches according to the intensity of our purpose in life.

If you are satisfied with smallness, you will have smallness appearing as your satisfaction. Your satisfaction will always be as grand as is the intensity of your claim to satisfaction. If you are engaged in the joy of Being, then others will say, "How come you are satisfied and I only have satisfaction spasmodically?" You can say, "How come you have fallen for just any map that leads to the City, or to the Source of that State in which satisfaction reigns, where man sits and is found in Fact?" You see, nothing can be revealed about the place of the treasure unless you are willing to enter a new ship, a new state of mind in which to engage the seas of your experience. You cannot expect to find what I am talking about by remaining on the level of being a gadabout. You cannot expect to understand what I am talking about if you remain looking at the vision I portray through the dark glasses of egotism.

You cannot possibly see what I see, unless you look as I look beyond the eyes of limits. Know full well that you only perceive what IS according to your freedom from objective limits. There are many who need an object to say they desire until they find that in the fulfillment [i.e., in the accomplishment of deeper perception and understanding of what IS], the object is no longer an impediment to the fulfillment, but is the evidence of the fulfillment, because "All that I have is thine." The object as just an object is there to satisfy those who need a marking on the way.

To think that possessions are going to give you a sense of satisfaction points to a very interesting experience, because you will think that the more you have, the more happy you will be, or the less you have, the less happy you will be. This is no standard to go by. Someone once said to me,

"Mr. Mills, your home with all its beautiful objects must be such a care. It must be such a concern, such a worry for you." And I said, "Not at all. I know beauty, and thus I am constantly amazed at the various forms it wears. It is beauty that looks after beauty."

People think through the limits of their minds, and consequently think that all beauty for a "spiritual" man must be limited to a fast-like diet and a stringent-like existence, and that he must behave like a clam! "I may speak; I may not speak. Step on my bed and I may squirt you," says the clam. "Step on my territory, and you will know where you are. You will see my hidden presence because I cannot help but defend what I think is mine!" You cannot say that the clam is unconscious; you can only say that the clam is not aware of being a clam. It merely responds to the pressure existing around it, and it moves, opening and closing, according to the tides of time.

This is somewhat like men and women. They usually don't realize how mechanical their territorial defensiveness actually is. They are so at home in certain types of "beds." We never consider that the reason our beds are hidden is that we, like clams, must rest unseen. We must always have our sleeping chambers, and they are considered very private because we do not want others to intrude or to know what we look like when we resign ourselves to sleep. We can cover our faces with creams and oils with the hopes that we don't dry out overnight! We can cover our heads with hair curlers so that our hair will be curled in the morning in case our experiences during the night have not curled it (and invariably they don't!). We can have our bed chambers completely private from the rest of our living experience, because in those moments when we renounce our objects and our own objectified bodies, we give ourselves unto the Unknown and yet Known. We know that in the state of sleep, we approach the periphery of such a satisfying State that we appear rested upon awakening to another day. It is not that we have found ourselves; we have just been freed for a time from the mind of thoughts about ourselves!

My talking about a Lalique vase with birds on it will never give you the experience of seeing the Lalique vase with birds on it. It will never give you the opportunity of holding the Lalique vase with birds on it. It will never give you the *experience* of the Lalique vase. It will only point to the experience. This is like realization. Realization of the Lalique vase is accomplished when it is perceived, felt, experienced. Then you perceive that the crystal and the design are only the forms that beauty and its art have utilized in expressing an idea of transparency. If you leave the piece of crystal on your table, you will only have, perhaps, one vase, but if you are cognizant of the Light behind the vase, your knowing may appear to kindle every man's wish to perceive such a vase of beauty. They may then find and claim one that is becoming to their level of perception, to their level of appreciation of art and its objectified beauty.

To consider only this side of existence in order to gain the Other Side of existence is unwise. This side of existence points only to what is on this side. The Other Side of existence, however, when considered, may offer a view that reveals this side of existence to be an array of symbols, which when understood, can bridge the gap between this side and That. Usually, you can only bridge this gap of understanding by the use of symbols. Remember, too, that the eventual bridging of the gap only happens when there is a transcendent experience. A merely intellectual perception of symbols is not such an experience. Intellectual perception is all wrapped up in the ego, and unless the ego and intellect come to meet their Maker, in other words, the undisputed Point (which the intellect and the ego cannot eradicate, regardless of any bleach!), you find yourself amid the Age-old dispute that has arisen between intellectual perception and the inner, intuitive penchant for transcendental experience. This penchant always transcends what the intellect deems to be within the realm of possibility. The intellect and "you" go well together. The intellect and "I" do not meet. I AM That which I AM. You are what you are. I AM That which constitutes my Am-ing. You are this which constitutes your expression. I AM That which I AM because I AM constant. You are this which you are, changeable, because "you" is the result of change. I AM constant. You are change.

Now, you can bridge the gap: if I AM constant and you are change, and you realize through experience that the "I" of you never flickers in the change of you, then you realize that I am always in change, but I AM never touched by the changing! You can appear to be always satisfying the need of those around you, provided you remain as I AM and know no need [i.e., as real] to satisfy.

The art of living beyond the three-dimensional sphere of this world and its inhabitants is to live in that state of Awareness or Consciousness in which the Self experience illuminates the three dimensions. Despite the objects, objectifications, and the objections of time, this state of Consciousness is able to point to the timeless Shore where there is no clam squirting in the mud flats. Only the Pearl is revealed on that Shore where understanding reigns. Here, you stand revelling in the revealed Truth, as Being is found freed from the shell of belief. The shell of the clam of belief has two halves: one shell is mind, the other shell is body. The same kind of shell houses the oyster, but the oyster knows enough to use its irritation to produce a pearl. A clam only uses it to persist in remaining in the mud flats!

In the early days of my speaking, one horrified woman one day said to me, "I do not believe you use a very fine symbol when you speak of the oyster and the pearl, because the pearl comes as a result of irritation!" It was so interesting, as soon as this one was irritated, I never saw her again. She never did realize the lesson that the oyster taught. The oyster has taught men to realize that irritation is no malady if you are willing to use it as a means to understanding Reality. If you were really satisfied as you are, you would never feel limited as you are. If you were truly satisfied with your obvious appearance, you would find that your satisfaction was based on the *size* of you! So, everyone would be putting all present manufacturers of scales of weight out of business because of the great extent to which everyone would be increasing their satisfaction-poundage. They would think that the less pounds they had, the less satisfaction they would have! But we know very well that the type of weight that is termed "personal satisfaction" bears little responsibility toward those who are crying out, "Give unto me, Sahib, the satisfaction that you have in so much abundance, that you have in so much presence. Give unto me, Sahib, of your treasure."

Satisfaction does not depend upon your condition. Satisfaction is the garment that is worn by one who bows to the Infinite. Such a one is found declaring, "In this am I satisfied, in this am I glorified, and in this am I found in the springtide [i.e., the rhythm of newness, new birth], which brings to man's awareness the intrinsic powers of Being." As the spring festival brings Easter to bloom, one dances between tulips/two lips. Many men and women know that through the two lips they partake of a fine table, they partake of a fine wine, they partake of gastronomical delights at astronomical prices. Through the two lips men have tried to tell of the wonders, but they can never tell through the two lips what they are if they remain nothing but bulbs in the mud of time. The two lips are forever trying to drink from another the mysteries of union, but I tell you now, the mystery of fulfillment is not found in trying to take from another, to drink from another, to find in another. The great power of Union brings the realization that as I AM All, there is no "other." In this realization am I satisfied, in this realization may I engage another, and in this realization may I marry another, but in this realization I AM forever *single* in fulfillment.

I have never been against marriage. I have never been against anything. What you call "against," I always think of as an opportunity to *gain*. You see, when you think you have a chance for irritation, it can be a gain. It is not *against* anything. It is a gain, because when you have irritation, it can either move you to find what can eradicate the irritation, what can free you of the irritation, and in the healing you find the balm, perhaps, of the Christ.

No matter what religion you have been given, no matter what rock you have found to be sacred, no matter what stone you have named as the one capable of being rolled away, the central, universal Factor of all faiths is Awareness, which enables you to perceive all these happenings. Do consider what you translate the symbol of the cave or tomb to mean in which Jesus' body was placed, waiting to be transformed, transfigured, and laid to rest in the peace that passeth understanding. The dawning reveals the state of Consciousness wrapped up in the "I" and not wrapped up in the mind-body of a Jesus or a Gautama.

The Light behind a Jesus living as a power is the realized Self, called the Christ. As was the case with Him, those on the way may not know you any longer, they may not recognize you any longer, because by your vibratory frequency are you known, not just by your embodiment. And your vibratory frequency has changed greatly. You create an *impression* by what you add to your outside, but you are an *expression* of what has been given to you as an accomplishment within. It is one thing to wrap the body in linen and to cover it with oil when you sleep, but it is another thing to take it up renewed in the Eternal Day of the Irradiance becoming a resurrected State termed a risen or elevated Consciousness.

The whole purpose of the Eastertide is that everyone parade in a garment of such fineness that they all make a flocking to find what each other looks like when they are clad in the unlimited resources of an imaging fashion plate. Easter is not just another time to earn or spend a "fast buck" at an Easter sale in order to be in vogue. There is no sale on Easter, there is no merchandise to be had, there is no sale of the Christ, there is no cheap sale. But it is a costly experience to come face to face with an indisputable situation in which the Christ supreme appears to fulfill the desires of the heart and walks as an experience among men. You would not be partaking of an innate prompting to get beyond your limited satisfaction if it were not to find the unlimited, satisfied State of Being, in which desire and its heat has faded into accomplishment and its gain.

The whole power of any experience rests in your ability to translate it from the literal to a meaningful experience beyond the confines of mental explanation. If I strike you with a ruler, you can say that you were struck by a ruler. But no one but you knows the experience. By hearing the description of being struck by a ruler, you think you know, but only you who have been struck would really know the experience. If I jab you with a point, you may cry "Ow!" And you would wonder what caused that one to cry "Ow," but only the one who experienced it would know. Yet, you would say, "What is 'Ow'?" And you can say, "An impersonal happening that was a result of a realization when it struck me unaware." Usually, when awareness dawns it's "Ow!"

It is like intuition. I have been asked frequently, so many times, about intuition, as if we already understood what thinking is! But intuition bypasses thinking. Thinking is so slow. Intuition does not depend upon your thinking. Intuition is the act fulfilled, which thinkers later describe. People will say, "How did you know to do that?" And you will say, "It is an act appearing fulfilled, and all I can say is that my tuition was paid when I died to being solely a thinker and found my Soul the Am-ing of the Being I AM."[1]

You have there an example of a vortex of power that can cause anyone to sit in a cave, in the opening of a place of power, and perceive from the heights how the waters meet and wash away the adamantine conditions of the time-mind. If water will carve a way through the face of a mountain, what hope we do have, for it points to what Light can do in the twinkling of an eye. Water takes centuries to carve a masterpiece. Light takes a moment to reveal the Master at peace. Time and action wear away obstructions; Light reveals instantaneous atonement, at-Onement.

A Tone met when claimed [i.e., the authentic Spoken Word], pitched to a vibratory frequency of universal significance, can enable you to tap the root of your experience, leap beyond being a vegetable, and find yourself able to partake of any food, for in the Master Light, food is not considered to be either good or bad. It is only known as the evidence of the sustaining power of the Infinite. To think that diet is going to free you from your state so that you can become more "spiritual" is just another one of the maps that pirates have sold—and they have been pretty bold! If you think that by eating meat you will have more sex energy, or by eating vegetables you will have less, you will find, if you try either, that you will still be bound to your own original condition. Yet I tell you now, if you feel a great sex drive, it is marvelous. At least you have got some energy to have to do something with! I have found so many people who do not seem to have any energy that the question of what to do next never has to enter their thought! That seems to be the condition of people in this city. No one seems to have enough energy to know what to do next. There isn't enough.

The people in this area seem to be so satisfied with living in the confines of a sun state, but are rarely expressing Sonship. People are forever acclaiming this area as an opportunity to live in the sun, but they never say,

---

[1] "Tuition was paid" refers to the immediate knowledge that intuition makes available.

"In this state you may also die in the shade [i.e., ignorance]!" Many realize that there are supposedly all kinds of paths to God, but few have perceived that there are not all kinds of Gods. Everyone seems to have his own *idea* of God. But when you perceive that there cannot be all kinds of Gods, when you touch the hem of what the true One God-experience is, then you realize that what you *conceived* God to be was merely a temporary conceptual crutch. You used it until you found that you no longer needed it. You see, what you give unto God as sincerity, constancy, humility, and fidelity in relation to the Cause for which you came [i.e., God-realization], you will always find returned unto you many fold. You will never again find yourselves struggling against the tides of time. You are flowing with them. The River of events is moving between the great banks of your humanhood. Unlike those who dwell in isolation, you will find yourselves once again looking up and flowing with the River, and in this act, you will find how the River supports you on its way.

To step into the River is to find yourself witnessing unto those who are being baptized in its waters, and who are engaging an initiation into the Rite of Light Experience. Men and women are once again looking for a promise to be fulfilled according to the Scriptures of Light, which has been promised by the Prophets of Light. That Promise states that all men will once again walk in the Light, as the Light, and be a light upon a hill, not set apart, not concealed under the bushel basket of thoughts, but freed so that they would enlighten every man his way.[2] Each step you take should not just be a step into or out of a mundane situation; each step should be a step into the rhythmic act of Beauty:

> Beauty, beauty, undefiled
> Can never be caught by an errant child.
> Beauty, beauty, undefiled
> Walks as Light beyond all miles.
>
> Beauty, beauty, undefiled
> Can never be thought in terms of time,
> For it is found as Art supreme
> When man would dance beyond his dreams.

So, in this rhapsody of wonder, praise, and expectancy, may you perceive so simply that the maps of time that point to the treasure chest of gold may be enticing to the adventuresome spirit, but do know that if your

---

[2] Matthew 5:14–16.

treasure is found only in the objectified gold bullion, it is deemed wise to share it with the source from which it came. You can always keep the other half. It sounds like a wonderful bargain, but I tell you now that when you stand before the Bar of the Light, the only gain is found when you realize the the Gold of the Sun is never up for sale, is never lost beneath the waters of the unconscious, is never hidden from the sight of one who is filled with desire, intention, and purpose. You see, the same energy may appear on the lower plane as desire, on another level as intention, on another level as purpose, and on another level as fulfillment, for in this you are moving, not toward the experience of objective gold, but toward the appropriation of subjective Light. You must realize that in the apparent act of appropriation, a tremendous change comes over you.

You cannot succeed if you just *think* you know. Experience demands change! You may appear to be a different character or you may always appear to be the same person, but your power will move from one trying to carry power through the personality complex to one carrying power involuntarily by knowing the Point. May you come to understand the fact that ends were never made to meet. Beginnings were only made for ends,[3] but as I find the Point, I know that the beginning and the ending are only for those who have forgotten the indelible Point that has written the story of fulfillment upon the scrolls and maps of Consciousness.

> When you lay yourself down and you find you arise
> In the dawn when the sun graces the sky,
> When you find the sphere decked in birdsong,
> And you find you have passed the night e'er long,
> You find in the dawn, in its rays of might,
> The birds chant the way to open to Light.
> The birds mark the way, for without cause to sing,
> They chant their praises to the unseen Power as King.
>
> In this song, like a melody supreme,
> It awakens each dreamer who would be freed of dreams.
> And may your feathered friends give you wonder in sight
> And cause you to close your eyes and see Light.
>
> In that moment you find, in the magnitude of grace,
> That the Masterpiece of Light dawned. Do you know the Face?

---

[3] "Beginnings" and "ends" are best understood here as meaning birth and death. Dying believers can never come together and recognize their common, known Life.

> Have you seen the sculpture of those who have tried
> To more and more be beyond the limits of hides?
> Have you seen how they've tried, with form all around,
> To define the space in which they are hide-bound?
>
> But the feather of bird in its garment in time
> Enables *your* feathered friend to pen a melody divine.
> For his beak dipped in liquid gold of Ray
> Elucidates the Promise in a warbling way.
>
> May you find, as you come to a Tone sublime,
> You say, "This Bird gave it to me, and I take it as mine.
> And in this taking I find this fact
> That when I sing my tone, I know the fact
> That the root of the tone is the one found in the Song of that Bird,
> And this may I chant, and by this be heard."
> In such a Song of power you can hear the Sound
> When you find the wonder on a branch seen, and the Wonder
>       ungowned.

It is one thing to desire the things of God; it is one thing to want to know the things of God; it is another experience to be what God IS when freed from "you." In That, find how you are freed from "you," and in That be satisfied. I AM the same yesterday, today, and tomorrow, even though we appear to sleep, for in That State we rest knowing that the "I" forever watches and witnesses unto our own continuity. The Light dawns as realization for those who would witness unto the perfect Day. There is no purpose of a Buddha, of a Jesus, or of any Master if you think entirely within the framework of person. A Buddha, a Jesus, or a Master is never understood from the standpoint of pieces, but only from the standpoint of the artless art of involuntary Being defined.

What you will make out of the Unfoldment will be according to the depth you wish to plant yourself in Light ground. You can take this message and analyze it, criticize it, silently anaesthetize it, and live as if I hadn't spoken it. Or you can attempt to live it according to how you think I have spoken it, which refutes the whole purpose of my speaking it. You see, the whole purpose of speaking it is to give into sound a translucent, transparent vehicle that is both formless and formed, which can transport you into a higher understanding of Consciousness. It is experience upon experience, revelation upon revelation, that gives you the opportunity to leap from one transparent stone of Truth to another, witnessing but not falling for the dualism of time. If you know the Point, you bear within yourself the power to voluntarily appear among men and women in order to be the custodians of satisfying satisfaction and the evidence of captives set free.

You are the living evidence of captivity led captive. You see, when you have once searched for the higher meaning of life, you find "All that I have is thine." "Seek ye first the Kingdom of God, and then all these things shall be added unto you."[4] But do not seek the Kingdom as one who would search out a treasure. Do not go "treasure-hunting" for the Kingdom. The treasure, the great golden chest, of course, is the Kingdom of Heaven. Do not attempt to search out this treasure chest or this heavenly state of Consciousness in order just to get things, just to get satisfaction, just to find happiness, just to find beauty. Seek first only the Kingdom of Heaven. This involves attempting to meet the demands of God-Being. By this you will fulfill the exigencies of Light. "Let there be Light," and in that letting, go; and in going, find; and in finding, Be. Involuntarily be the offering unto this great crescendo-ing wave of new birth clad for a moment's celebration as Easter.

---

[4] Matthew 6:33; Luke 12:31.

# Foundation of Vision

*Analysis
is in vogue today
primarily because people have lost
the God-Man-Self
vision.*

# 18 Foundation of Vision

April 24, 1979, Arinaka, Tucson, Arizona

This is the morning of April 24, 1979. I was reading a statement I made on April 6, 1979: "How can you move or move people if the personality is in such conflict with the movement?"

I think this is an interesting statement, because it seems to be so applicable today to so many situations. How can you move if the personality is in such conflict? I guess the whole question comes right down to: "What company do you keep?" You see, if you are in conflict with your movement, then you must be keeping the wrong type of company [i.e., company of people, company of thoughts].

What is the point of your experience if it isn't to find situations that are going to enhance you? It's the same thing with friends. It's the same thing with associates. What type of associates do you have? What type of association do you have with your associates? So often we don't have very much in common, and we should have everything in common.

I was very moved this morning by thinking about ideas that have to do with association and how we are spending our time. Are we choosing wisely? Are we really choosing to be with people who are supporting our cause to Be? Are we associating with situations that will cause us to be more in tune with our purpose, our goal, our aim?

I wonder if we are really concerned about being in the correct company. I wonder if we are really concerned enough whether or not the company is pushing us beyond the mystical experiences of saints and pushing us into the lap of the Sage. I wonder if we are really choosing the correct situations to enhance our actions. You know, it has been said that you'll never be a fine tennis player if you just play with somebody who is your equal. But very few people want to play with anyone better than they are, because most people who are better are egotistical and they like to show off what they have accomplished technically at your embarrassment. They know very well they're better than you are. But it takes great humility for them to play as if they weren't better and to place their shots in such a way that you start to experience what it is to play better and better tennis.

I wonder if it isn't the same thing with us. I wonder how many of us associate with people who are going to make us respond to the serve correctly. I mean, don't let your dander get up because somebody serves you a very fast ball and you miss it. You don't throw your racket down and walk off the court, even if you lose game after game. But we do this so frequently in our life experiences. We get our backs up over nothing and then don't hear what is being said.

And so, correct association is very important in society. As water seeks its own level, so should you seek the level of inspired associations — associations that are going to enhance your purpose. Then, we should consider what we are doing to prepare ourselves to associate correctly. You can't associate successfully with a physicist if you don't know what the word "physics" means. You can't associate with an historian if you don't know there is such a thing as history. So, how are you going to associate correctly with those who are dealing with Life if you don't realize that there is such a condition beyond the living? To be able to perceive that condition requires a life factor that is missing among most living creatures. That missing factor is the ability of the creature to look at itself.

This is something you seldom consider. The ability to look at yourself is the greatest gift you have above the level of being beasts. The beast is what constitutes our appearance. And yet, we all behave as if it didn't. We are always trying to deny the beast nature, the animal nature, and this is how we get all tied up. You have to be able to face what you are really like and look at it without emoting about it. Look at it as if it were somebody else. You must develop the ability of stepping beyond yourself. The ability to step beyond yourself enables you to look at yourself and not be afraid of what you're looking at.

[Mr. Mills sneezes.] It is so delightful and so satisfying to sneeze in the face of dust! But who ever heard that dust could cloud the vision of the Infinite? Even if you move dust around, who ever heard of a particle of dust interfering with the sight of the Infinite?

This great ability to look at yourself is essential if you are going to move anywhere, because if you don't utilize this awareness, this ability to look at yourself, you will continue to remain in the throes of society as it is at present. It is so important, because to be able to look at yourself and to see whether or not what you are looking at conforms to the Ideal enables you to divorce yourself from the dwarfing and thwarting effects of false identification.

The room is very quiet. Often your quietness is an exclusivity that is due to an unwillingness to face yourself, see yourself, and be the Self. To be perfectly quiet in the classroom with a living answer is folly, unless you always wish to remain nothing but question marks! Instead, why don't you claim to be an exclamation mark after the word *eureka,* which means "I have found"!

All of life, as it seems to be, is based on organic involvement. All of Life, as it truly is, is founded on the fact that Awareness is intrinsic to being, even human. The Awareness that dwells as the conscious experience of being human is the same non-material Power or Awareness that is intrinsic to God-Being. The bridge between this and That is Awareness. The first prerequisite of experiencing the totality of Awareness is to be able to *see* yourself. Only then can you hope to enter the Temple via the gate of knowing yourself. To see yourself is to look upon your experience; to know yourself is not to have knowledge of what isn't, but to have understanding, which frees you from knowledge. Knowledge of itself is a catatonic state. Understanding brings it out of suspension.

What did I say to you at breakfast about knowledge and understanding?

>Jaan K.: You said, "Understanding enables something to live, and knowledge keeps it in a catatonic state."

One of the very interesting things that is missing today in our society, in our group, and in our experience as it seems to be is vision. So, we're talking about how to see ourselves. Why is vision so important? The saints were visionaries, but their vision had to be freed from personal involvement. Vision is a marvelous tool to contain and to maintain in the face of a society that is destroying itself. If you can destroy a man's vision, he becomes blind. If you can destroy a group's vision, it becomes aimless. If you destroy a society's vision, it becomes wide open to exterior domination.

The tendency of this present Age, as some great thinkers have pointed out, is that each man is claiming a tremendous amount of time and space in "doing his own thing" to the detriment of himself and others. You see, without the awareness to view his acts from an impersonal standpoint and without the foundation to know how to change them, he is perpetually going back and forth between the two unfixed states of personal thoughts and personal emotions. This perpetual attrition is what weakens the entire structure of a man's social involvements and his encounters in living.

The imperatives of today are wrapped up in "analyze the situation." "Let's have the critical analysis of everything that we're seeing today and bring it before a table of bored people so that they can go on boring holes...." "Bore a hole, bore a hole, right in the sugar bowl, and wonder, 'Who did it?'" No one but those who are themselves in bits and pieces. That's what analysis does to people. And we wonder why they have such a propensity toward alcoholic involvement!

In such an overripe stage of fermentation, we have had to call upon those who would attempt to sort out the various thought patterns and thought forms so that they may be looked at by the mind [i.e., referring to psychiatrists and psychologists]. But you must understand that analysis has arisen because the Light has seldom been recognized. Consequently, the possibility of experiencing Light has rarely entered the vision of those who were to lead. Ramana Maharshi[1] was a great Light. He held the vision of God-Man. People from all over the world found his Light glowing because one man wrote about him in a constructive way. This man was Dr. Paul Brunton.[2] By his writings, the doors were opened for many people who were serious about finding the Self.

The Self is uncontaminated by analytical theories of the mind. Analysis is in vogue today primarily because people have lost the God-Man-Self vision. People who have not lost this vision know that one day they will be able to see beyond the horizon of limits. Mankind has been kept attuned to the Higher Mystery of Life by the influence of those who have kept such a vision alive. It has been the sadness of many to see how those who would discount vision have destroyed attempts by others to maintain vision. In destroying vision, we are a people walking in darkness. But by recognizing that we are walking in darkness, we immediately know there must be a great Light, because otherwise we would not know that we were walking in darkness.[3] Then, in seeing the glow of this great Light, we are besieged with a

---

[1] Ramana Maharshi was an enlightened Sage who lived in India. He was born in 1879 and died in 1950. He attained Enlightenment at the early age of seventeen and left a concise but rich heritage of spiritual writings. The essence of his Teaching is the discipline of "Self-enquiry," carried out by the conscientious and diligent questioning of one's identity: "Who am I?"

[2] Paul Brunton was born in London, England, in 1898. He is well known for his clear and illuminating writings on Eastern philosophy and religion. Among the many Sages and holy men he has encountered, Ramana Maharshi was perhaps the most significant. Owing largely to Dr. Brunton's writings, Ramana Maharshi rose to worldwide recognition in his time.

paradox: how can there be a coincidence of the human and the Divine?

People who lose their vision are open to suggested visions [i.e., illusions]. The greatest hope that many people have today is for a unification of people, world, governments, and banks. But you see, if such a suggested vision is only based on knowledge, the vision dies, because it is understanding that enables the facts that knowledge holds to be given life. You can only expect to experience a unified world if it is built on the foundation that is termed the Source of all possibilities: the staking of the claim to one's innate nature as a Conscious Being.

If we do not work from the foundation that "Consciousness is fundamental" and that "I am in the Father and the Father is in me," which is the same as "I and the Father are One" or "I AM That I AM," how are we ever going to engage a vision that is without bias? You can only see the same view if you look from the same point of view. You can only engage what another sees if you are willing to look in the same direction. This "sameness" is not the loss of individuality; this "sameness" is the open door to finding the Individuality that has never been lost. The only thing that can be lost is the counterfeit individuality, which can never really be found, because it was made from a false cast, it was never real.

You cannot create authenticity by mimicking a counterfeit vision. The authentic vision is "one world," yes, but first of all "One-God-Man-World." You must persist in holding the vision of God-Man in the realm of critical awareness, and you must not be seduced into the critical analysis of the counterfeit. If you hold fast to the vision of One World and One Man in the image and likeness of God or the Self, you will find that the United World as the Symphony of Soul can be realized.

The great question today is not only "With whom do you associate and keep company?" but also "With whom are you being what you really are in the light of a living answer?" You can never be successful by your own instruction. You can only put off the inevitable experience of dying [i.e., dying to limits] by your degree of entanglement in the analysis of the mind's products. The whole purpose of High Teaching is to alert you to jump beyond the coffin of the mind and stand on its lid and find it to be a springboard into the Awakened State. The Awakened State is one in which you are consciously aware of being free of the pitiful entanglements associated with the thoughts about being a visionary in time. From the standpoint of Being, you are able to

---

[3] Matthew 4:16.

carry the vision of God-Man unto all men and women of all nations, races, and climes.

Water seeks its own level. The mountain that is crusted with snow and gleams by its crown of ice cannot withstand the natural effulgence and warmth of the sun. The snow melts, and in its melting forms water that fills the canyons and the rivers and then flows into the sea. The great circle of Life is uninterrupted, regardless of the appearance of catatonic states. Knowledge is like what is frozen on the peaks of human attainment. Understanding we find as we are exposed to the warmth of a living Sun/Son experience.

In this great circle of movement, you will find the Point that enables you to view the world ever-changing and men and women ever-sparkling as they don garments of time, mind, and space that are befitting to the demands of the Age in which they find themselves. The Truth of Being has always been the same. Yet, the difference between yesterday and today fools you, because you look to time, space, and people in order to see what states are about, instead of looking to "C" and finding the Christ vision the one that opens the door. The great sea, the Red Sea of suggested might,[4] parts, as do the clouds of suggestion in the stroke of a conscious act directed to quelling those events that could halt or appear to hinder the natural flow of the One Divine Event termed Love's chant of praise. This chant says unto the heart prepared, "Take this note and find its meaning. In finding its meaning, understanding will grace you with a smile, and in That, revel."

In the experience of transformation, which causes others to declare, "In this appearance you are changing," you can dance in the sheer delight of knowing. It is inevitable, because I AM nothing other than what I AM, the beloved Self of my own God-Being. In this I am forever satisfied with the vision of Life as it IS, music as I AM, and the world as a tone on the string pitched to universal significance. The world must once again be plucked from its orbit of limits and given back to the crescendoing might of awareness freed from entanglements and mindfulness, as men and women don the infinite Robe of Self Conscious Experience.

In this may you find the Rest that is filled with meaning and the

---

[4] On p. 549 of *The Metaphysical Bible Dictionary* (Unity Village, Montana: Unity School of Christianity, 1931), the Red Sea is described as follows: "The Red Sea represents the sum of all the thoughts about life with which the race has impregnated the universal ether. In the mythology of the Greeks and the Romans this is symbolized by the river Styx, over which souls were ferried by Charon. It is familiar to metaphysicians as the psychic realm or race thought, which has to be overcome by the progressive soul."

Silence that is pregnant with the power and the glory given unto the Fundamental Fact of Being. Know that "I" associate with the Root of all experience that is founded on the Fundamental Tone of the Heart.

My heart sings, my head bows in the light of a new Song.

This Age in which you find yourself discounts vision and exalts analysis. Find yourselves the living experience of vision and thus open wide the door so that those may enter who would know the wonders of understanding, which set the captives of knowledge free. *Find!* And in finding, give; and in giving, receive. May you know what it is to declare, "Now I know what it means to be free, unbound." The pinions of inspired might enable you to look down upon the mountain and upon the rivers as they find their way to the great Sea/C. In that Ocean of Wonder, find yourself riding the great crescendoing Wave of might as it crashes against the flimsy fortifications of the dust-mind.

In these words may you find how it may be recorded that we have spoken on this morning in the foothills of these sacred mountains in the presence of wonder and awe. As the vision unfolds, knowledge is not cast down, but set free in the understanding of the revealed Foundation of Being.

## The Electrical Force Field

*It is evident
what thoughts you entertain,
because you are the result
of the thoughts entertained.*

# 19   The Electrical Force Field

September 13, 1979, Sun-Scape Inn, Sparrow Lake, Ontario

This is the evening of September 13, 1979. I am meeting with a few of those from the Great Lakes area. The Great Lakes are like the five senses, you might say, and are all contaminated. It is interesting how the lakes are contaminated, as are the senses, by what we give unto them. We are the result of our thoughts. Do you realize that your appearance, your corporeality, doesn't point to anything real other than the Divine Idea called Body? You are the result of your thoughts, and it is evident what thoughts you entertain, because you are the result of the thoughts entertained.

It is very important to realize that you are creating your own miserable existence. You are solely responsible for it! No psychiatric treatment or electrical shock treatment in the institutions will really do you any good. A certain type of shock treatment that I know of may do you a great deal of good,[1] but the electrical shock treatments that some of you may have been prone to experiencing at one time can never do you any good. You pay for them, though; they are said to blow your "psychic web" [i.e., mental and emotional integrity]. They may also destroy many of your mental abilities. It is so unfortunate how some people have had electrical shock treatments to help bring relaxation to their turbulent conditions, which were primarily due to having blown their minds with drugs at one time. But most people do not realize that the principal drug is the personality. They don't want to bring their personalities into the Light of Principle, and consequently they disturb themselves. In some cases, they are completely aware that they are disturbing themselves. God has been so good to bestow upon us the incredible gift of perception. We can perceive ourselves and can often perceive what we are doing to ourselves. It is an amazing thing to think that we could ever get away with trying to experiment with His creation and understand the great mechanics of it via the very part of the organism that is itself so mechanical — the mind!

Thoughts, as you know, are manufactured, and they are con-

---

[1] Referring to the surprising situations that can develop in dialogue or confrontations with a competent Guide or Teacher.

stantly on an assembly line. They are constantly being tossed out into the world. In fact, one reason that you have so many disparate thoughts is that the entire area that we call space is nothing but energy waves. You see, thoughts are carried on energy waves, and the mind is capable of picking them up.[2] The reason we appear energetic and the reason we appear vital and the reason we appear dynamic is that we are existing in a dynamic, electrical force field, not a physical force field, but an electrical force field. This is why you people must consider very carefully what you are thinking. Your thinking is up to you. You can be careless and entertain whatever thoughts you wish. If you entertain the thoughts of being sensitive, super-sensitive, super-colossal, a super-duper dope, or a super-duper witch, go right ahead! Go right ahead, ride your own damn broomstick if you want to, but with that attitude, instead of riding it, you should have it broken over you, at which point you should be made to sit on the splinters!

    The important point here is coming to you in a very simple way: your sweetness, your sourness, your rhythmical actions, and your unrhythmical actions are all results of what thoughts you choose. If you want to be obstinate, you choose to be; if you want to be arrogant, you choose to be; if you want to be pleasant, you choose to be. It's not recorded that you will be this way or that way; you have to *choose* the record. You programme yourselves to be miserable and you are miserable. You programme yourselves by the thoughts you choose and entertain. Everything that you are doing and everything that you are entertaining now is what you will have to live through tomorrow. Everything. God is good, so they say, but you can see what your minds do to you.

    Your whole experience is created by you, not by me, not by anyone but you. If you are feeling miserable, it is because you yourselves are entertaining the thoughts of misery. That is why some of you sleep so much. When you are asleep you don't entertain the thoughts of misery. Often, you will daydream and entertain what you would like to have happen. Or, if your life is dull and you want a little extra spice, you can sometimes get it in your night dreams. A lot comes to the surface then. Some people can actually reach you through dreams. But don't pay too much attention to dreams. A dream is as much an illusion as this waking dream is. In fact, there is nothing real about the waking dream, but look how you have suffered by trying to perpetuate it. The only real thing about it is the Light behind it. And the Light often

---

[2] Mr. Mills continually warns his students about this possibility. He often says, "Be sure you are thinking your own thoughts!" Also, he warns his students about the harmful effects of thinking negative thoughts, because they can be transmitted to others.

manifests as electrical impulses that tickle more than your funny bone [i.e., that transcend the mundane]. That is what enables you to laugh, to crack a smile (and sometimes hurt your face!). That is what enables you to enjoy yourself in spite of yourself. The electrical force field in which you live often triggers certain things within you at times that your mind is not quite capable of decoding.

Any of you who have had the delicious experience of indulging in your miseries, give them up! If you have been graced by having been given much, the only evidence of your success will be in how much *you* give back as a result. That is the only way to keep the stream flowing. Don't be a dammer. So many of you are obstructionists. Your profession is "obstructionism." Being an obstructionist is often characterized by the futility of getting in the way of something that is going to mow you down sooner or later anyway! One thing that is going to mow you down sooner than anything else is the shenanigans that you try to perpetuate with a false sense of accomplishing something from the wrong premise.

Anything that you accomplish that is well done from a premise that is personally oriented just points to the fact that there is something more to you than what you think. Everything that you think gives you everything you see, and that is where your freedom ends. Where your progressive thinking stops is where your limits live. Yet, you are too often hemmed in by your limits of misguided thoughts. I have often said that the Urn of Aquarius is being lifted and its contents are pouring down upon you in your regions of thought. What is it pouring down upon you?

Students: Knowing.

Yes, knowing. And why is knowing important? Knowing is not confined just to the visible. Knowing is not confined. Knowing of the highest order enables you to have the Invisible and the visible at your disposal to be utilized according to the path you have chosen.

Now, a thinker always loves to be in a stew. A knower always loves to sit on the ledge, waiting for some trembling of the earth (perhaps caught in the grips of a rhythmic laugh) to drop him into the Abyss.[3] A *knower* implies that "you" can know. A *knower* personalizes his knowing. That is why you make so many mistakes as a knower. You call that mistaken name,

---

[3] The "Abyss" refers to the region beyond knowledge, approachable only when the personal self, that is, the knower, is superseded.

or mistaken identity, a "knower." A misnomer. Mr. and Miss Nomer. A new marriage: Mr. and Mrs. Nomer! Mr. and Miss Nomer. [laughter] Isn't it going to be awful, when you go to bed with your spouse tonight, you won't know what you're in bed with! Know very well that your senses cannot tell you what she or he really is. Oh yes, it is incredible what you presume! [laughter]

What are we dealing with? An electrical force field. You see, you have to be very careful of how you are "charged." Positive or negative, you are always searching for other "filings" that are on the loose that may be attracted to you. Of course, if you are on the loose and you are trying to find someone else who is on the loose and who you want to get tied up with, you are supposedly trying to mate, or in other words, match. And what is a match going to do? It is supposed to equalize, stabilize, and bring balance.

But you see, people don't live in balance or in peace; they live in stew. Matching is supposed to bring balance. What is the point of balance? The point is that you don't lose it. But how do you know you have it? You can't think you have it. You know you have balance to some degree when your thinking has taken you as far as you can go and you move onto the line of knowing, which transcends instantaneously the point to which thinking would have led you only after a long time.

Knowingness moves in the company of intuition, and thinking moves in the company of mechanical men and women. You will never find men and women without the mechanics of thinking, but you can find some men and women who are capable of bearing the children of knowingness.[4] And that is, of course, what you are here for. You are all the progenitors of children of knowingness. You cannot behave as if you weren't. You all are people bearing the gift of knowingness.

Now, do not think that you are going to get anything out of marriage that you have not already got now. That is an illusion of marriage. Another problem is that marriage has no more mystery to it. It never has had a mystery to it, really, outside of the fact that the bride was usually considered to be a virgin. And of course, we don't even know what the word means today, outside of virgin soil or virgin country, God's country!

But you see, the mystery has gone. And what has gone with

---

[4] That is, thoughts, words, and deeds that are birthed as a result of a higher understanding of Consciousness.

mystery? Wonder. And what has gone with wonder? Everything that is at the base of the experience of transcendency. Marriage should be that state in which, when you unite, you know you don't. Then you *die* to each other and have no more "freedom" whatsoever! Anyone who tells you that when you are married you will each have plenty of elbow room is selling you a lot of baloney. They say the institution is just great: "Appear to be married and have your sex when you want to, but don't fence each other in." Go on with you. It is exactly opposite. When you marry, you do not have the right to be what you think you want to be. You have to do what? Balance. So many marriages are not successful because there is no balancing. Often partners won't balance. One partner wants the other to do it all, and that is not fair. I mean, who wants to be a juggler all his life? That is why so many people take to tipping the jug! It is so true. I know it.

Marriage has nothing to do with thinking. Marriage is what you are before you think you aren't. Marriage is what? The state of union beyond all stripes and stars! [laughter] Yes, that is why governments are having such a time—they are all in labour! And those periods of protracted labour are called union strikes. Union *strikes*.[5] [laughter] That is why they have to try to move things a little farther than mere table talks. A table talk is what happens when you have forgotten Who is the Star and what is the talk. The table talks are usually psychic investments, of which governments are usually made up. Isn't it amazing, isn't it a grace that you can go to sleep and forget all about them. It shows you how they are made up![6] Governments will always be in turmoil, and so will nations, as long as they are populated by dreamers. The purpose you have in this year of the Light is to be an alarm so that people will have the joy and privilege of experiencing a jolt when they think too much about getting together to be happy. So many people feel that by getting together they are going to be happy. Happiness results not from the ability of you people to get together. Happiness is the experience of what it is to be together before you get together.

The trouble with all unions is that they come to a table in order to

---

[5] Unity has impact!

[6] The mark of Reality is permanency and unchangeability. Anything not permanent is unreal and therefore like a dream, like something "made up." The point made regarding forgetting about governments when you sleep is that governments are not permanent, that is, permanent in your awareness when you sleep, which denotes their unreality. Only that which is permanent in one's awareness at all times, regardless of the waking, sleeping, or dreaming modes of mind, is real. That is the Self.

try to head off a breakdown. If people would only get off the head, there would not be any breakdowns. If they would treat their heads as they do the head on a stein of beer [Mr. Mills imitates blowing the foam from the surface of a glass of beer], there would be hope! After all, what would beer do without hops? But what will you do without a skip and a jump?

      I will tell you now, as long as you have static on your line, you will never have love. Love is not a static state. You would like to make it that way, but it isn't. Most people find that love, instead of being the power that lifts you out of you and your thoughts, is a situation that garments two people trying to make something out of nothing and only boiling the bones of contention amid the tears of emotion, yet salted by the grace of E-Motion [i.e., Eternal Motion], which points to the Energy that is electric but short-circuited by the lack of grounding.[7] This may put all psychiatrists and psychologists out of business, because the only trouble with all patients is that they think too long. People were never meant to think too long. Three score years and ten, well, maybe twenty. People think too long. Three score years and ten is the maximum time you have for thinking. After that is when you may start to live. Real living is based on knowing.

      Thinking has to do with being peaceful; knowing has only to do with Being. Who wants to be a petunia in an onion patch? One of the cats I once had was crazy over onions, and I'm telling you, if she had liked garlic, we would have had to send her out to one of our neighbours! Cutest cat you ever saw. When it reeked of onions, we called the onion the cat's "mickey finn." Doesn't that knock you for a loop?

> Pamela H.: I think that most people in this room, Mr. Mills, don't know what a "mickey finn" is. It's a knock-out drop that is placed in somebody's drink to render them unconscious.

What is the "mickey finn" you all take and yet expect to know me? It is the ego-drop. And when there are too many of them, they are called "drips." And when there are too many drips, they form a lake. Water points to the emotional state. There is not a thing wrong with emotions. The only thing wrong with them is that you don't *do* with them. You let them *do* with you. You don't know what to do with them. Instead of becoming oriented to the waves of the E-Motion, you try to swim in the stew of your personal feelings. An emotion is nothing but the name given to an electrical impulse that holds

---

[7] Personalization is the lack of grounding that creates the short-circuit.

you in its grip as you forget the Source. An emotion is the sign that you have much at your disposal to utilize with a purpose. And when you don't utilize it with a purpose, you have what is known as stew!

Yes, Peter. (Don't use that recipe for anyone's meal!)

Peter C.: You made a statement on January 18, 1973, sir, six years ago, that I feel is so appropriate for this evening. I was just beginning to memorize it before you came in. You said, "Man is the rhythmic pulsation of an energy field that is commensurate with the Power That IS. That Power, in an attempt to be known, may be called Love."

The things that are significant are so seldom seen when they first arise. They should be recognized and enjoyed at the same time! I look at all the books today that are on the shelves in libraries. I think of all the great lives that have touched ours in moments of wonder and awareness. In fact, our awareness would not be what it is if it were not for those who have held and who hold a very high level of awareness present as their lives appearing to be lived. It is very interesting to see these books and to realize that these people who live and who have lived were as unsung as we are today. Of course, most people today who have a message to give are seldom really recognized, because a real message recognized reveals a New Land, a New Government, and therefore a New World, a One-World. And there is great resistance to this. This is why the whole world is in such a state of fermentation.

In the depths of humanity there is the seed of knowingness that you are more than "meat" and therefore more than thinking, which goes with meat. There is no value in thinking unless you associate. Do you realize that *you cannot hold a thought unless you associate with it*? I found this in my notebook. I don't know whether I got this from another book or if it is something that unfolded to me while I was reading. But what does it matter? We do not die. That Which IS does not; that which isn't does. And you will find that the evidence of Light, of Truth, of Wisdom, of Joy, is forever bearing its own testimony as it chooses the lives that are to be lived according to the great penchant of the Heart, sometimes called the Source, God, or the Self. The realization of said Source or Self is wrapped up in a sound called "Christ." It is not a name, it is a frequency: *Christ*. "Jesus the Christ" is only the way *we* say it.

We are dealing with language. Language is like a line that is strung as a result of mentality, upon which may be pinned sounds wearing garments called words. Remember, your language is your means of communicating with each other, but it is also the means for transcending the belief of twoness in the Light of Oneness. You are not a little bit of God. Some of you may look as though you are pretty big pieces of God, but you are not! [laughter] You must realize that your person really has no influence whatsoever. It doesn't show you what you are at all. It just points to what you are wearing. You are aware of thought and have associated it with a form. Remember, thought is an electrical impulse. It is an electrical wave. You experience that electrical wave and dwell in a realm in which a form is aligned with it. You call it the "human form." But as soon as you start destroying the correct thoughts about the form, you are destroying your possibilities of continuing to live in this form. Some of the most destructive thoughts are jealousy, envy, pride, selfishness, egotism, lack of response, lack of expression. These are detrimental to your form. Willfulness and obstinacy will also destroy your form. Why are we told to love and to do unto others as we would have them do unto us? Because by doing so we are utilizing the Power to the form! And this is where the real attraction lies. It isn't just for the "meat." Real attraction is in the knowing of what thoughts are found acceptable in the Light of the Ideal.

This is why the High Teaching states that you should choose those thoughts that are in keeping [Inn keeping] with the high state of Christhood, because the mystery is this: As a thinker you die, but as one knowing One, you appear to fulfill the plea of the mass. In knowing, you can service the visible and the Invisible with equal acumen and wisdom. You find every moment an auspicious one in the fulfillment of the Grand Plan.

No wonder opens the door to boredom, and boredom is the doorstep to breakdown. Breakdown is the result of not counting down your blessings. To "count down" your blessings enables you to jump, when the moment is at hand, over the suggestions that would bind you. May you be found in the Promised Land. I remind you now of a mystery: "In a moment, in the twinkling of an eye, at the last trump . . . we shall be changed!"[8]

What is the mystery of "we shall be changed?" The mystery is revealed in the realization that in the light of your sense testimony, you can entertain angels unaware, and they are winged unto your presence in sound. It is wonderful and really so glorious to perceive that certain books [i.e., of a religious nature, such as the Bible] have recorded and held man's greatest

---

[8] I Corinthians 15:52.

promises and potentials, but it is sad to realize that time has almost always yielded victory to the grave-mistake.[9] We know that as we live in thought, so do "I". But even though we die in thought, "I" do not. As we live in knowing, we change and find ourselves clothed in the new garment commensurate with our realization of Union and the understanding of all the demands of this great Force.

The table is prepared, the discourse has been offered, and the dessert has been shared. Here we are in the dessert of this Meal, having found this Place [i.e., state of Consciousness] in the pristine wonder of sound [i.e., the words spoken] due to the unfathomable wonder of a Power not known, yet experienced and called the "electrical field." We live and move and have our being wrapped in its rhythm. Without rhythm, life would have no ability to appear as a possibility among the dreaming dead.

Life IS; living appears. "I" live, for I AM not a thought. You and what you associate with in thought constitute you and your world. What "I" know lives, and that is the Light World of Conscious Experience.

How to talk about the intangible, invisible Existence amid the tangible and striped conditions of time, where the stars have been painted on your flags—but you have not known, and thus the flags are only waved over the various states of humankind in order.[10] But what is that order? The true order is that rhythm and harmony bring a melody, a pause, and a rest. In this order, Man appears as the Power, and men and women experience inspiration and an unlimited dynamic flow in the stream where Love is said to be all. Oh, what a task to be a living awakener! Oh, what a joy to see dreamers springing beyond the reach of time's suggested limits and finding, in the timed appearance, the wonder that the Timeless wears, which appears as the light to a face, the sparkle to the eyes, and a Crown of Glory for those who know that "He cometh to claim all his jewels, precious jewels, his loved and his own."[11] The bright Crown adorning—oh, if you ever see it, you will be in awe, and having seen it, you will understand the Almighty Will Eternal.

---

[9] The books have reminded man of his innate unity with God, but few have realized the Promise and have thus died in ignorance—the grave-mistake.

[10] For instance, in the United States, the sequence of each state's entrance into the union. The point being made is that world governments are only a substitute for the Government that is on His shoulders.

[11] A line from a well-known children's hymn.

No greatness has ever died. It is only the smallness of thinkers that has led you to believe that it could!